# What's Good about This News?

# What's Good about This News?

## Preaching from the Gospels and Galatians

### David L. Bartlett

Westminster John Knox Press
LOUISVILLE • LONDON

*Book design by Sharon Adams*
*Cover design by Pam Poll Graphic Design*

*First edition*
Published by Westminster John Knox Press
Louisville, Kentucky

This book is printed on acid-free paper that meets the American National Standards Institute Z39.48 standard. ♾

PRINTED IN THE UNITED STATES OF AMERICA

03 04 05 06 07 08 09 10 11 12 — 10 9 8 7 6 5 4 3 2 1

**Library of Congress Cataloging-in-Publication Data**

Bartlett, David Lyon, 1941–
    What's good about this news? / David L. Bartlett.
        p. cm. — (The Lyman Beecher lectures)
    Includes bibliographical references.
    ISBN 0-664-22526-8 (alk. paper)
    1. Bible. N.T.—Sermons. 2. Sermons, American I. Title. II. Series.

BS2341.55.B37 2003
252—dc21

                                        2003050084

For Carol, with all my love

# Contents

# Introduction

This book represents an expansion of the Lyman Beecher Lectures delivered for Yale Divinity School's annual convocation in October 2001. Because of the renovation of the Sterling Divinity Quadrangle, now blessedly completed, we actually held the Convocation Lectures at nearby Bethesda Lutheran Church. Chapters 1, 3, and 4 are expansions and revisions of the lectures as I delivered them. Chapters 2 and 5 have been added as a further exploration of my theme for the purposes of this book.

I have deliberately kept something of the oral style of the original lectures. I hope that they read the way I talk, at least when I have worked hard on preparing what I have to say. I have decided not to omit or play down the life setting of the original lectures. One piece of the social context I knew when I accepted the invitation to deliver the lectures. The Divinity School convocation of 2001 was part of the tercentennial celebration of Yale University, and at the end of the week, after delivering the lectures, I audaciously delivered the sermon to mark the celebration of the Tercentennial Weekend.

The social context for these lectures that none of us predicted was the painful crisis of September 11, 2001, a crisis that was still vivid in our memories when convocation began less than three weeks later. I reshaped much of the lecture material in the light of the events of September 11, and I have not pretended to change that material in the light of more recent developments. What I said then may be less immediate now, but I hope it is not less pertinent.

After teaching preaching on and off for many years I have discovered that one thing, and often *the* one thing, my former students remember about my lectures is that I tell them that preaching is always good news. Preaching is news; it is fresh, involving, surprising. It is not the repetition of tired formulas or one more self-serving plug for whatever program the deacons or the denomination have voted for that month. At the very least, therefore, I remind our students, preaching is a lively word. It is not a sin to be interesting.

There are important continuities in the way good news is understood throughout the New Testament. It is still always the herald's announcement of God's victory. That victory is always won through Jesus Christ. But what the good news looks like and how we respond to that good news is different for Matthew than it is for Paul, and different yet for John's Gospel and Mark's and for Luke and Acts.

I hope in these chapters to suggest what gospel might look like in each of these strains of the New Testament. Here is what gospel looked like for Paul. Here is why he thought his gospel was good news—the nature of the victory he proclaimed. Here is my best guess on the nature of the congregations for which he wrote. Then on to Matthew, Mark, Luke–Acts, and John.

But I want the book to be suggestive and not just descriptive. And I hope we can do at least three things with these suggestions:

1. We can decide which strain of good news is both good and new for our congregation in its situation. Some churches may need to hear more about the freedom of the gospel with Paul and others may need to hear more about responsible living under the gospel with Matthew. In any church where I have served (and in the divinity school where I teach and preach now), there are weeks when Paul's word seems just the right word and weeks when it is Luke who is the herald of just the news we need to hear. Faithful preaching will discern what is different about the sermons we preach on Paul from the sermons we preach on Acts, and it will seek to discover and suggest where gospel can be found in each.

2. We can learn the ways in which the different strains of the New Testament do understand good news somewhat differently, and we will probably discover that we cannot hold on to them all with equal fervor. The diversity of the canon shapes and reflects

the diversity of the church. I hope that as a preacher you will be able to name and know your own central convictions and to learn from the Scripture that feeds them.

3. And we can learn from those strains that are less central to our own theological understanding the correctives that help us realize and declare the richness of God's Word. Sometimes when we preach on perspectives not easily congenial to our own deepest convictions we will want that tension to be part of the preaching. Sometimes we may discover as the years go by that the biblical book that seemed less helpful to us turns out to provide just the perspective that we need.

## A Word about the Sermons

One of the first things I tell students in Yale's Principles and Practice of Preaching course is this: preaching is occasional. That is, a sermon is not written for all times and for all places, but for this time, this place, this gathered group of people. The purpose of preaching is to give a word that is needful or at least helpful for that day, to sustain people through the week ahead. The preaching that I like to do the most is preaching to people I know the best—to the congregation I serve day in and day out.

Harry Baker Adams puts it powerfully:

> The preacher is responsible both to the word that God has declared and to the community in which the word is to be spoken. Preaching is not simply reporting what God has said or done; preaching is making known what God has said or done so that it can be heard and appropriated by the people . . . in this particular place at this particular time.[1]

My decision to work as a divinity school professor these past fifteen years has cut me off from that regular preaching to a congregation that has called me. However, two of the congregations represented in the sermons that follow come close in some ways to being my own flock.

The Divinity School community celebrates worship five days a week in Marquand Chapel, and one of these sermons was preached for them for the Friday Eucharist service. Yale University celebrates public worship each Sunday morning at Battell Chapel, where I once worshiped regularly and now still worship occasionally. One of the sermons was preached at Battell for a community Good Friday service. I thank Chaplain Frederick Streets for the invitation to preach on that occasion. Both at Marquand and at Battell I know many of the congregation members, and I live with the same issues, in much the same context, as the others who worship there.

The sermon on Matthew 25 was preached just as 1999 was coming to a close and people were thinking about the coming millennium, which, whether it really began on January 1, 2000, or on January 1, 2001, was celebrated among us as 1999 turned to 2000. The congregation at Central Baptist at Hartford was also dealing with the retirement of its longtime senior minister, just two weeks before. It is a church I had preached at from time to time and, like the last church I served as a pastor, it is an urban, multicultural church. It is also a church of my own denomination. All this is reflected in the occasional nature of the sermon.

The sermon on Mark was preached at the First United Methodist Church of Wichita Falls, Texas. The sermon was followed over the next four evenings by four lectures on the Gospel of Mark. The occasion was the annual Perkins Lectures at the church, and I am grateful to Elizabeth Perkins Prothro and the late Charles Prothro and their family for endowing these lectures and for their warm welcome, and to the Perkins Lecture Committee and Pastor Robert Allen for inviting me to be there. The sermon tries to do what I think Mark's Gospel does—introduce curious people to Jesus as Mark understands him.

The sermon on Galatians was preached at South Church in New Britain, Connecticut, an American Baptist and United Church of Christ congregation. I had preached a few years before as the church celebrated the anniversary of its union. This time the assignment was specific: to help the congregation think about joining the Welcoming and Affirming Churches of the American Baptists and the Open and Affirming Churches of the United Church of Christ. After the sermon preparation was well under way I discovered that during the service where I was to preach the congregation would celebrate a family's adoption of three children that week. The sermon was followed by a Bible study and discussion about the issue of openness. My convictions on this issue are clear: I support openness to gay and lesbian persons in every aspect of church life, including ordination. I wanted the sermon, however, to raise the larger issue of unity in the body of Christ, and I wanted the discussion to be a real discussion. The issue of openness is one I have been dealing with openly since 1976—and perhaps this is the place and time to acknowledge that I would not have spoken out so early or so steadily without the urging of Randle Mixon, who, like St. Paul to the Galatians, has therefore been a very *aggelos* of God to me. (See Gal. 4:14.)

At some points the sermons, most of which were preached before this book was written, will recapitulate themes from the book. I tried in vain to decide whether these are "typical" of my sermons. In form they are not among my most daring, and perhaps in content not the most surprising. They do try to do the main thing: proclaim good news to God's people on the basis of a biblical text.

## Acknowledgments

I am deeply grateful to Dean Richard Wood and the faculty of Yale Divinity School for inviting me to deliver the Lyman Beecher Lectures and to Dean Rebecca Chopp for presiding over their presentation with energy and grace. I was honored beyond words to be able to present the lectures to a gathering of my family, my colleagues, both present and emeriti, Divinity School classmates, clergy who had become friends through the years, and present and former students who came to cheer me on. I am reasonably sure that Jean Bartlett is the first person to hear both her husband and her son deliver the Beecher Lectures, and I was especially grateful that she could be there. Carol Bartlett read the lectures in advance and made her usual wise suggestions. She and Benjamin and Jonah are the great gifts of my life.

Stephanie Egnotovich has long been both editor and friend, and I thank her and Westminster John Knox Press for their encouragement from the beginning and their nagging at the end. It was at the suggestion of the Press that I have added "sample" sermons to the book, with a few words of context for each sermon.

Colleagues and students through the years have set me thinking about many of the issues raised here. In particular I thank Harold Attridge and Adela Yarbro Collins for their wisdom on John's and Mark's Gospels respectively. Harry Baker Adams was my first preaching teacher and continues as inspiration and guide. Three Yale students have given considerable effort to helping my research and my writing for this book—Christopher Jarvinen, Frederick Simmons, and John Vonder Bruegge. I am grateful to them all.

Before I began the lectures in New Haven I said a prefatory word, which I repeat here:

> Some years ago when Leander Keck had to postpone his Beecher lectures and I was one-fourth of the backup team, I remarked that the first time I came to Yale Divinity School it was to hear my father deliver the Beecher Lectures from the high pulpit in Marquand Chapel.
>
> When I discovered that this year we would have the lectures in this splendid setting at Bethesda, I was only slightly disappointed that I would not be able to stand where my father stood. But in the far more important sense, I hope I stand exactly where he stood: for I am not ashamed of the gospel.

David Bartlett
New Haven, Conn.
October 2002

*Chapter One*

# The Good News in Galatians

## Introduction

In one way or another, every preacher knows that what she preaches is supposed to be the gospel, and most members of the congregation have at least some sense that the gospel is what they've come to hear. Although they are called "Gospels," we know that the gospel is not confined to the four books at the beginning of the New Testament. Paul talks at great length about the gospel and about his gospel, and faithful people have found gospel throughout the Bible, from Genesis to Revelation.

The term "gospel," *euaggelion*, which the earliest Christian writers used as a description of the Christian message, may have been a word they borrowed from the surrounding culture. There the term referred to a message delivered by a herald, sometimes the message of a royal birth, sometimes a message of military victory. It was an announcement (an *aggelion*), and it was a good announcement (a *eu-aggelion*).

Adela Yarbro Collins and J. Louis Martyn point out that in the larger culture to which the early church belonged, the news of the emperor's success was usually indicated in the plural, "glad tidings" *euaggelia*, while Paul—like Mark and other early Christians—uses the singular "glad tiding." Whatever the etymological importance of this distinction, there is no doubt that Paul thought his glad tiding, his good news, to be singular in its importance and universal in its scope.[1] Just as Abraham had only one seed, Jesus

Christ, God had only one tiding, though of course that tiding had implications and applications deep and broad enough to fill the world.

Or it may be that early Christians noted the Septuagint's use of the verb "to declare good news" as a translation of Isaiah's verb *bashar*. So, for instance, in Isaiah 40:9 the prophet declares, using the participle of the verb: "Get you up to a high mountain, you who preach good news to Zion; lift up your voice with strength, you who preach good news to Jerusalem. Lift it up, do not fear; [and then the content of the good news:] say to the cities of Judah, behold your God!" And the Septuagint picks up the same verb "to evangelize," "to gospel." If this is the history of the word "gospel," then perhaps Christ and Christian preachers stand in the line of the great prophet who declared God's presence and coming deliverance to people in exile. Brevard Childs points out that in Romans 10:15 Paul explicitly makes use of the nominative form of *bashar* found in Isaiah 52:7. "And how are they to proclaim him unless they are sent? As it is written, 'How beautiful are the feet of those who bring good news!'"[2]

In any case, in the New Testament Mark says that Jesus began his ministry by calling people to believe in that good announcement, and in Galatians 1:11–12, Paul says that he is a minister or herald who brings that announcement:

> For I want you to know, brothers and sisters, that the gospel that was proclaimed by me is not of human origin, for I did not receive it from a human source, nor was I taught it, but I received it through a revelation of Jesus Christ.

Paul also says that there are teachers who claim to be bringing the good announcement, but actually are preaching another gospel. Then he corrects himself: there cannot be another gospel. Either there is good news or there is bad news. What he preaches is good news and what his opponents preach is bad news, in every way:

I am astonished that you are so quickly deserting the one who called you in the grace of Christ and are turning to a different gospel—not that there is another gospel, but there are some who are confusing you and want to pervert the gospel of Christ. But even if we or an angel from heaven should proclaim to you a gospel contrary to what we proclaimed to you, let that one be accursed! As we have said before, so now I repeat, if anyone proclaims to you a gospel contrary to what you received, let that one be accursed! (Gal. 1:6–9)

Now as I first planned this lecture some time ago, I moved here into a somewhat jaundiced analysis of what has happened to the idea of good news in contemporary America.

Not much of what is called news is newsworthy, said I. And not much of what is deemed newsworthy is good. I talked about the triviality of media news, especially TV news, and noted that even on a sunny day our local television station calls its weather segment "Storm Center Eight."

But then of course the real storm broke, and for the first time in a very long time both the network that we watched and our local station presented, with great restraint and dignity and sympathy, news, real news.

Real news. Real news is news that changes the way we think about ourselves. On September 11, 2001, the news was that we were more vulnerable and less self-sufficient than we had seemed.

Real news is news that changes the way we think about our neighbors. I think that for every one on 9/11/01 the neighborhood got larger. Not just for those of us in Connecticut, but across the nation and across the world, Manhattan and Arlington and Pennsylvania seemed right next door and the victims and their families felt like our families too.

Real news is news that changes the way we think about history. The fatuous belief that somehow we had entered into an era of unstoppable American triumphalism got stopped, dead in its tracks.

And for the faithful and the seekers, real news is news that changes the way we think about God. Or more richly, real news is news that changes the way we relate to God.

My little analysis of the death of news, full of clever asides and condescending observations, suddenly seemed as trivial as the happy news it criticized. We no longer have to worry whether people know what news is. News is what changes the way we think about ourselves, our neighbors, human history. News is what changes the way we relate to God.

Now we only have the deeper worry: Can any news really be good news?

Our news can be good news—not easily; not cheaply; not stupidly. But still what it was meant to be. Both news and good news.

As I noted in the Introduction, often what my students remember about my lectures is that I tell them that preaching is always good news, fresh, surprising. It is not the repetition of tired formulas or an announcement of the church's agenda. At the very least, preaching is a lively word. It is not a sin to be interesting.

Because preaching is *good* news, I nag new preachers not to nag. I urge them to try the following experiment: Try preaching a sermon that does not once say "we ought" or "you ought" or "we must" or "you must" or "let us remember that . . . ," which is always just a veiled rhetorical way of saying "we must."

Hidden not very far behind this exhortation to go light on exhortation is my longtime devotion to the study of St. Paul, and, as my former parishioners will attest, my almost obsessive habit of preaching, not on the Gospel lesson, but on the Epistle where, I have long suspected, gospel is more explicit than in the Gospels. For the first years of my pastoral ministry I was unencumbered by the restrictions of the lectionary, and in those years especially I turned almost slavishly to Paul's reminder that for freedom Christ has set us free. Martin Luther wrote that Galatians was his Katharina von Bora, and in many ways Galatians was my Carol Bartlett, my heart's home.[3] During those years one of my parishioners was the distinguished Christian ethicist and theologian James Gustafson, and it came to pass after one of my more impassioned Pauline sermons that Professor Gustafson made the following literally unforgettable remark: "There's no question where the center of the canon lies for you. What we need now is some Matthew to balance your Paul, some Wesley to balance your Luther." I returned to my study to weigh these already weighty words, and picked up my study Bible to begin the planning for the next Sunday's service. As I picked up the aging Revised Standard Version of the Bible, there fluttered forth from the binding and landed on the desk exactly and only seven pages—the entirety of Galatians, the poor epistle worn out from overuse.

On that day I became a lectionary preacher and have only occasionally wavered from my commitment to the discipline that the diversity of the lectionary provides. Behind the practical decision was an important theological realization, underlined by Professor Gustafson's wry reminder. Within the treasure house of Scripture there is a diversity of gifts (if the same Spirit). Put in other terms, while we always preach the gospel, what counted as gospel for Paul in writing to Gentile Christian Galatians is a little different from what counted for Matthew in writing his Gospel for a Jewish Christian congregation in, say, Antioch. (What counted as gospel for Paul in writing to the Galatians was also a little different from what counted as gospel when he wrote to correct the excesses of the Corinthians.)

There are important continuities in the way good news is understood throughout the New Testament. It is still always the herald's announcement of God's victory. That victory is always won through Jesus Christ. But what the good news looks like and how we respond to that good news is different for Matthew than it is for Paul, and different yet for John's Gospel and Mark's and for Luke and Acts.

### What Was Going On in Galatia?

Not surprisingly, I need to begin at the beginning.

Confessionally, let me confess that for me the beginning of a fuller understanding of why gospel was good news came in my reading of Paul. And when it comes to the New Testament, any understanding of what makes gospel gospel has to start with Paul as well.

Historically we do not know who was the first person to use the term "gospel" for the Christian account of the way God deals with humanity in Jesus Christ. We do know that some time before Mark wrote the first "Gospel," Paul referred consistently to the message he proclaimed as gospel. Not "a" gospel, but "the" gospel.

We know that he thought what he preached was "the" gospel, because when some other Christian preachers followed him into Galatia and preached their variation on the message about Jesus Christ, Paul at least rhetorically starts to grant that there might be other gospels, and then almost immediately takes it back. Paul Schubert, who was my teacher at Yale, reminded all of us that Paul usually began his letters by telling the recipients how grateful he was for their faithfulness.[4] Galatians begins quite differently. Notice the unthankful tone of the passage we have already cited:

> I am astonished that you are so quickly deserting the one who called you in the grace of Christ and are turning to a different gospel—not that there is another gospel, but there are some who are confusing you and want to pervert the gospel of Christ. But even if we or an angel from heaven should proclaim to you a gospel contrary to what we proclaimed to you, let that one be accursed! As we have said before, so now I repeat, if anyone proclaims to you a gospel contrary to what you have received, let that one be accursed!

So strong are the words that Hans Dieter Betz thinks that Galatians is a kind of magical letter. If you read and obey it, you will be blessed; if you disobey, you will be cursed.

> Galatians begins with a conditional curse, very carefully constructed, cursing every Christian who dares to preach a gospel different from that which Paul had preached and still preaches, different from the gospel which the Galatians had accepted. . . . By including this dimension of magic, Paul

*repeats* the Galatians' initial confrontation with the gospel. His letter is not merely a piece of rhetoric, but it is composed in such a way that it functions at the same time as an efficacious display of the divine Spirit and Power.[5]

We can sketch only briefly what this "other" gospel that Paul's opponents preached may have looked like. The best sketch by far is found in J. Louis Martyn's commentary. Let me take just one aspect of his description of the Christology of Paul's opponents. Martyn calls the opponents "the teachers," and I choose this passage because it captures so many of the themes Martyn sees in the opponents' teaching:

> We can be sure, above all, that [the teachers] consistently avoid every suggestion that God's Law and God's Christ could be even partially in conflict with one another. In their own terms, they are presumably certain that Christ came to fulfill the Law and the prophets (cf. Matt 5:17–18), perhaps even to complete Moses' ministry by bringing the law to the Gentiles. For them the Messiah is the Messiah of the Law, deriving his identity from the fact that he confirms—and perhaps normatively interprets—the Law.[6]

My one puzzle about Martyn's fuller sketch is the oddity of Paul's apparently having to tell the Galatians that if they take on circumcision they take on the whole law (Gal. 5:3). I cannot make this work with the claim that the teachers were already loading the whole law on the backs of the hapless Galatians. We are a long way from Paul and a longer way from the teachers (whom we meet only through his polemical description), but I am helped by Alan Segal's claim that, oddly, Paul is still a more rigorous Jew than his opponents. As a Pharisee he believes that if you take on the Torah you take it on rigorously—no halfway measures for lifelong Jews or for converts either. If these Galatian Christians want to undertake the law, then Paul says they had better take it on the pharisaic way: hook, line, and ritual stipulation. Paul is saying that as

Christians the opponents are too rigorous, but that as Jews they are too lenient.[7]

This, then, is my guess on the situation Paul faces. After he has preached a gospel that claims that faith is central, exclusively central, to the shape of the Christian life, other teachers have come in and argued that the God of Jesus Christ is also the God of Moses, and that the way to enter into relationship with God is not only through what God has done in Christ, it is also through the ways in which we are obedient to some of the laws of Moses.

## Paul's Gospel

How do we understand the one and only thing that is central to Paul's gospel? When Luther fell in love with Galatians, it was because Galatians says as loudly and clearly as possible that we are justified by faith alone (whether our faith or Jesus' faithfulness may not end up making as much difference as we might think). I am too much an heir of that claim to let it go—even for a minute. If we let go of this central claim about God's righteousness, there is the constant danger that we will think that Paul's gospel is first of all good news about us, and not first of all and above all good news about God.

Acknowledging that, nonetheless, I want to explore Paul's gospel claim using slightly different images than the forensic images of justification, images also there in Galatians. I do this not to preach another gospel, lest I be cursed, but to understand that same gospel from a slightly different perspective. I do it for homiletical reasons, thinking that if we read the same text with slightly different lenses, it may preach more freshly for us, this year at least.[8]

I want to think about what it means to be part of Christ's family. If Luther's great concern was how a sinner might be made righteous before a righteous God, Paul's great concern was also how Gentiles and Jews might be members of one covenant community, one family. (This does not mean that what Luther found in Paul wasn't actually there; it just suggests that it wasn't the only thing Paul was thinking about.)

How could Jews and Gentiles be part of one family for Paul?

The short answer is that all were children of Abraham through faith, and all were brothers and sisters of Christ through adoption.

Abraham Malherbe sums up the Pauline understanding succinctly:

> New relationships came about as a result of conversion and baptism. Paul understood the experience of the Spirit in conversion as a change from ignorance to a knowledge of God. This knowledge was expressed in the new self-understanding that the believer was a child of God, but that experience was to Paul possible only in a new community. In his interpretation, the Spirit baptized Jews and Greeks, slaves and free, male and female, into one body (cf. 1 Cor. 12:13). The baptismal language in Gal. 3:26–4:6 represents the convert's initiation into the Christian community as an adoption by God through which the convert is admitted into a new family of brothers and sisters.[9]

All are children of Abraham through faith. Paul's great proof text is Genesis 15:6, which said that Abram had faith, and it was reckoned to him as righteousness. Whether Paul had come to believe in justification by faith and was delighted to find a text to support his claim, or whether he discovered in Genesis 15:6 the language to declare the grounds of Christian family, text and claim come together. Abraham was reckoned righteous before God established the mark of circumcision; he was established as righteous before Moses handed down the law. He was declared righteous through faith, and his family is the family of those who imitate him by also being faithful (Gal. 3:6–9).

What is striking is Paul's unusual thinking about how God constitutes God's family. For Paul neither Jews nor Gentiles are children of God through the inheritance of the flesh. Abraham doesn't have seeds, the people of Israel; Abraham has one seed, Jesus Christ. And Abraham's seed is God's own son—in our terms one might say, God's biological son, though Paul's understanding of all that would have been quite different from our own. Yet through Christ all those who looked as though they were no longer God's family (the people of Israel), and all those who looked as though they had never been God's family (the Gentiles), become God's family—not through the flesh of genealogy but through the spirit of worship and faith:

> But when the fullness of time had come, God sent his Son, born of a woman, born under the law, in order to redeem those who were under the law, so that we might receive adoption as children. And because you are children [Jews and Gentiles alike], God has sent the Spirit of his Son into our hearts, crying, "Abba! Father!" So you are no longer a slave but a child, and if a child then also an heir, through God. (Gal. 4:4–7; similarly see Rom. 8:15–17)

(Other early texts read "an heir of God through Christ." Paul should have said this, even if he didn't.)

My wife and I have friends who have a wonderfully mixed family, mixed in part because one of their sons is their biological offspring and the other children are adopted. Not long ago they were explaining to the youngest child what it meant for him to be adopted—how he had been chosen, and waited for, and welcomed with joy. As part of the story they also had to explain that Mark, the brother, was their child biologically. When they had finished explaining what it meant to say that Tommy was adopted, he cried out: "Oh, that's wonderful. Can't we adopt Mark too?"

Paul believes that God has adopted us all, Jew and Gentile, male and female, slave and free, in Jesus Christ. And Paul declares the wonder of that adoption.

There is a great debate among New Testament scholars about whether when Paul refers to faith and Christ in the same phrase in Galatians he is talking about the way that the faithfulness of Christ brings justification, or the way in which our faith in Christ brings justification. It is an important issue, but it does not, I think, change the fundamental shape of Paul's understanding of the gospel. Through Jesus Christ, God adopts Jew and Gentile alike as God's children. Like Abraham we evidence, accept, signify, mark that adoption through faith. The faithfulness of God meets the faith of God's adopted children, and both the faithfulness and the faith are sheer gift, goodness, mercy, grace.

In my college years, like so many others of my generation I was much inspired by Paul Tillich's preaching, and perhaps especially by his famous sermon "You Are Accepted."[10] When I got to Yale Divinity School I discovered that among some of my mentors "You Are Accepted" was not accepted very well.

This was in part because the sermon seemed to provide easy access to cheap grace, though I think that complaint underestimated the way in which for many of us it was still both news and good news that there was any access to any grace whatsoever. The sermon was not accepted primarily because the phrase "You are accepted" seemed too watered down a version of Paul's great doctrine of justification by faith. Of course all we have is metaphors and glosses, and it may be that we do better to read Tillich's claim less as a gloss on the doctrine of justification and more as a gloss on the promise of adoption—of the way in which we become family.

At any rate, the sermon and my youthful affection for it came back to mind a few months ago when I was watching a British video on finding more effective ways to communicate with autistic children. The reporter was interviewing the father of an autistic son, a British construction worker, who, my guess is, had not ever read Tillich's sermon. The father was talking about how much his son felt cut off, estranged, alienated, disconnected. "What is it you would wish for your son?" the reporter asked. The father could hardly speak. Then finally, "I just want him to be accepted."

## Markers

Paul's opponents in Galatia are much concerned with markers. What markers? Markers that distinguish Christians from the larger pagan world from which they are now separated. Paul is also concerned with markers. What markers? Markers that make family family.

The opponents' markers are external markers—in Paul's terms markers according to the flesh. Circumcision is something you do to the flesh, and diet is something you put in the flesh. Paul's markers are markers according to the Spirit: you don't wear faith and you don't eat adoption. By the Spirit one believes in the promise: that's faith. By the Spirit one prays, crying, "Abba, Father!" That's adoption.

External markers divide the members of the community one from another. Internal markers (marks of family) bring the community together. Fleshly markers divide; Spirit-filled markers unite.

Think of the contrast between works of the flesh and gifts of the Spirit. Among works of the flesh are hatred, variance, emulations, strife, seditions, heresies. Among gifts of the Spirit are love, joy, peace, long-suffering, gentleness. (See Gal. 5:19–26.)

Put another way, the markers Paul protests are the markers that separate church people one from another: some are circumcised, some are not; some keep kosher, some do not; some keep Sabbath, some do not. That is why Paul gets so annoyed with Peter, who has been eating happily with the nonkosher Gentiles until James's allies come along, and then what God hath brought together, Peter tries to put asunder (see Gal. 2:11–14).

In our time there is both a strong and entirely honorable effort to hold forth the picture of the church's unity, and a strong and entirely honorable attachment to Galatians 3:28. "There is no longer Jew or Greek, there is no longer slave or free, there is no longer male and female." But we always remember that for Paul this unity is not a "natural" implication of the fact that we are all human. For Paul those markers that divide us lose their meaning because we put on Christ, who unites us. The great passage of unity ends with an appeal to the grounds of that unity: "All of you are one in Christ Jesus. And if you belong to Christ, then you are Abraham's offspring, heirs according to the promise." We are all one because in Christ God has adopted us all.

Note also that Paul does not for a minute think that membership in this family frees one from moral responsibility. The gifts of the Spirit also shape the life of the spiritual person. With good reason, Christians attracted to Paul have sometimes wanted to argue that his polemic against particular works of the law (circumcision and kosher diet) can be extended to an opposition to any sense that obeying the law, even the law about loving the neighbor, is part of the fundamental strategy of Christian obedience. The evidence on that issue is complicated and the exegetical arguments even more so.

What I think we can say with confidence is that in this letter where Paul is so concerned that Galatian Christians might think that keeping the commandment about circumcision might commend them to God, Paul suggests a quite different picture of the way in which Christ shapes the moral life. It is not so much that we discover in Christ the true shape of the law (though there is some of that), it is rather that we receive through Christ the gifts of the Spirit, and the Spirit shapes the conduct of Christians.

I do not think it is coincidence that when Paul talks about the way the flesh leads people astray he refers to the "works" of the flesh; and when he talks about the way in which the Spirit leads people right, he talks about the "fruits of the Spirit" (see Gal. 5:16–26). Life lived in the Spirit looks this way, not so much command as gift.

And after he has listed the gifts of the Spirit, Paul adds an odd phrase, which I'm not sure our translations get quite right: "There is no law against such things" (Gal. 5:23b). I am inclined to think that a better translation would be something like this: "The law does not deal with such gifts." Or, "When it comes to such gifts, we are not in the realm of law." (I know that Galatians 6:2 seems to go another way, talking about obedience as fulfilling the "law of Christ." All of which is to say, our easy categories may not work easily for Paul.)

At any rate we can be quite sure that Paul does not think that life by faith is life without constraints or guidance or obligation. It is rather that the Spirit shapes the faithful life more than the law demands it. The old saw is not a bad one when understanding Paul's moral exhortations: "Be who you are."

Last year I was watching one of the innumerable television programs that put commentators of quite different political viewpoints around a table and then invite them to yell at each other for half an hour or so. In this case the commentators were Mark Shields and Robert Novak, who have been yelling at each other in such contexts for many years. I forget the precise topic, but I know that at one point Novak said something to the effect that the poor people of Appalachia were poor because they were losers and had neither the ability nor the ambition to make it in our great American competitive society. Shields stopped him in midsentence with a very Pauline phrase: "Stop that. You're a better person than that."

Paul is always telling his fellow converts that they are better persons than they think they are. They live in the Spirit, and the fruits of the Spirit are "love, joy, peace, patience, kindness, generosity, faithfulness, gentleness, and self-control" (Gal. 5:22–23). Then he goes on to add: "If we live by the Spirit, let us also be guided by the Spirit"(v. 25). Be who you are.

## The Grounds of the Good News

Finally, it may be worth noting that in his letter to the Galatians Paul suggests the grounds for the gospel that he preaches.

First, there is the story of what God has done in Jesus Christ. God sends Jesus, Abraham's true seed, to take upon himself the curse of the law, so that those who have faith in him (or those who trust in his faithfulness) might be redeemed from the law and be adopted into his family. If, as I mentioned earlier that Betz suggests, Galatians is a kind of magical letter, threatening a curse on those who return to the law, it is clear that for Paul that curse should have been lifted on the cross, and to return to it is to return voluntarily to a kind of slavery. (See Gal. 3:10–14.)

Second, there is the Scripture, the Old Testament, which provides the grounds for understanding the story of Jesus. Paul can't tell Jesus' story without talking about Abraham in Genesis, and Sarah and Hagar, and Deuteronomy's curse on one hanging on a tree. Paul interprets those texts according to rules that seem foreign to us but were consistent with his own training, and we can assume with his sense of audience. At any rate, the gospel preaching he models is preaching that starts with the narrative of Jesus but reads it from beginning to end through Scripture.

Third, there is his own story. There are all kinds of reasons why Paul's reference to himself fits his rhetorical strategies and perhaps also the rhetorical models of his time. Homiletically he does what preaching has to do from time to time—make clear that he tries to walk the walk as well as talk the talk. He can speak of adoption into God's family because whatever his call looked like, it brought him into God's family through Christ in a way that his earlier law-keeping had not been able to do. He can speak of freedom from the dividing markers that make for separation in the church, because in Antioch he had it out with Peter around this very issue. (We all know Peter would have a somewhat different version of this story; and we as preachers, I think, should beware of anecdotes where we get all the best lines.) The reminder is that proper preaching sometimes is willing to hold up the congruence between the gospel that is preached and the way the preacher has discovered that gospel to be good news in her own life.

Finally, there is the experience of the congregation itself, and Paul reminds the Galatian Christians of some facts about themselves.

> They received the Spirit of God not through works of the law (they had not yet thought to take on circumcision and kosher table), but by hearing through faith. More concretely: they believed as they had heard Paul preach, and accepted what he said as good news for themselves (Gal. 3:2).
>
> They had miracles among them, not because they had taken on the yoke of the law (because they had not yet done so), but because they had received the Spirit through faith (Gal. 3:5).

> When they were baptized they laid aside the markers that distinguish Jew from Gentile, male from female, slave from free, laid them aside in the baptismal waters and emerged as new persons, Christ's persons (Gal. 3:27–29).
> When they pray, they say, "Abba," which means "Father," and because they say it truly, they know that they are adopted as Christ's brothers and sisters, as God's true children and heirs. And again when they do that they do it under the influence of the Spirit, not under the compunction to obey the law (as a gift, not a command) (Gal. 4:6).

I have a friend who adopted a young girl. Not an infant—a girl old enough to have her own doubts and resistances. The doubts and resistances were more than evident until that night when, tired and ill and needing comfort and assurance, the daughter cried out from the other room for the first time: "Mommy!" She was adopted, and she knew she was adopted.

> And because you are children, God has sent the Spirit of his Son into our hearts, crying, "Abba! Father!" So you are no longer a slave but a child, and if a child then also an heir. (Gal. 4:6–7)

Good news.

*Sermon*

# "What Counts"

GALATIANS 5:1–6

### I.

What count are the faith that binds us to God and the
love that binds us to one another.

Imagine a church: From the beginning it had been a Congregational
church, and in the way of Congregational churches it had fairly simple
worship: hymns, reading of Scripture, a sermon, community prayers,
the Lord's Prayer. Once a month the congregation celebrated the Lord's
Supper, and on some occasions they baptized infants whose families
and friends brought them to the font as a sign of faith.

Then a Baptist congregation decided to join the Congregationalists.
In the way of Baptist churches they were used to fairly simple worship: hymns, reading of Scripture, a sermon, community prayers, the
Lord's Prayer. Once a month the congregation celebrated the Lord's
Supper, and on some occasions they baptized adults, who marched
with the minister into the baptistry and were immersed as a sign of
faith.

Now this is an imaginary merger in a time far less tolerant than the
twenty-first century and a town far less progressive than New Britain,
so bear with me.

In the imaginary church the union started off quite well. Worship,
preaching, music, prayers—all came off beautifully, or as well as one
could possibly expect. But then came time for baptism. When the Baptists saw the first Congregational baptism, they were fit to be tied. "Too
young!" they mumbled as the parents brought the infant forward. When

Preached at South Church, New Britain, Connecticut, October 27, 2002.

the Congregationalists saw the first Baptist baptism, they were a little embarrassed: "Sloppy and unpleasant," they mumbled as the newly baptized adult emerged from the pool with a sopping robe and scraggly hair.

Nonetheless, there was no crisis as long as both groups said live and let live, or baptize and let be baptized. But a few of the Baptists were not satisfied. They sent out a congregational letter saying: "The only good baptism is believers' baptism," and they started boycotting infant baptisms altogether. More than that, they scurried from house to house in the town trying to persuade Christians who had been baptized as infants that they had to be immersed as adults if they were really going to be Christians.

Before long Congregationalists and Baptists were still listening to the same sermons and Scripture and reading the same hymns and praying the Lord's Prayer together, but they avoided each other at coffee hour and gossiped about the others behind their backs.

The pastor who had instigated the merger, we'll call him Pastor Paul, was deeply upset. He'd been immersed as an adult himself, and he thought that was just fine, but he actually didn't think God lost any sleep over how different people got baptized. What God did lose sleep over was a congregation of God's people that couldn't get along.

Pastor Paul hit on an idea and sent his own pastoral letter to this South Church, Galatia, Connecticut.

"Friends," it said, "I am astonished that you are falling away from the gospel. Even though you baptize differently, think of what you do together.

"Think especially about this: every week you sit down in the same meetinghouse and say the same words—'Our Father,' you say.

" 'Father' because of your faith in God. '*Our* Father' because of your love for one another as brothers and sisters in Christ.

"Listen," said Pastor Paul, "and don't forget. What counts is not immersion or sprinkling, not infant baptism or adult baptism, what counts is faith working through love.

"Faith that binds you to God. Love that binds you to each other.

"For freedom Christ has set you free. Stand fast.

"Love, Paul."

## II.

What count are the faith that binds us to God and the
love that binds us to one another.

We don't have to imagine this next church, because Paul tells us pretty
much all we need to know about it. Paul started this church. At first it
was a church made up almost entirely of Gentiles, Greek people who
had believed in many gods, but who came to believe in the one God
of Abraham and Isaac and Sarah and Jesus Christ. They gathered once
a week to sing hymns and hear Scripture and have a sermon and say
prayers and say the Lord's Prayer. From time to time they had the Lord's
Supper, and from time to time people got baptized. Because they were
Gentiles the men had never been circumcised, and none of the Gentile Christians worried about keeping a kosher table.

After a while some Jewish Christians joined the church. Because
they were Jewish the men had been circumcised, and men and
women did keep kosher table, and there was a little grumbling at
church suppers because the Jewish Christians couldn't understand
why the Gentiles would eat pork and the Gentile Christians couldn't
understand why the Jewish Christians wouldn't. But they managed to
get along.

Then some really zealous Jewish Christians joined the church. The
old motto of the church used to be, "You do it your way and I'll do it
my way, as long as we also do it God's way." The motto of the Jewish
Christians was: "My way *is* God's way." These Jewish Christians boy-
cotted any church supper where the casseroles included either ham or
bacon, and their leaders attended every meeting of the men's fellowship. After an opening prayer they always began a fiery monologue
insisting that their Gentile brothers in Christ should head to the nearest
rabbi and get circumcised before they came back to church.

The pastor who had started their church we'll call Pastor Paul,
because that was his name. He'd moved on to start other churches, but
he wrote a letter to South Church, Galatia, Galatia.

"Friends," it said, "I am astonished that you are falling away from the
gospel. Even though some of your men are circumcised and others are

not, even though some of you eat pork and some of you do not, think of what you do together.

"Think especially about this: Every week you sit down in Antonius and Claudia's house and say the same words: 'Abba,' you say, which means 'Our Father.'

" 'Father' because of your faith in God. 'Our Father' because of your love for one another as brothers and sisters in Christ.

"Listen," said Pastor Paul, "and don't forget. What counts is not circumcision or uncircumcision. What counts is faith working through love. Faith that binds you to God. Love that binds you to each other.

"For freedom Christ has set you free. Stand fast.

"Love, Paul."

### III.

What count are the faith that binds us to God and the
love that binds us to one another.

We don't have to imagine the next church, either, because Jane Rowe and I can tell you a good deal about it. We both worked and worshiped there for some years, a number of years ago.

The church was a typical American Baptist church in many ways. They had fairly simple worship: hymns, reading of Scripture, a sermon, community prayers, the Lord's Prayer. Once a month the congregation celebrated the Lord's Supper, and on some occasions they baptized adults, who marched with the minister into the baptistry and were immersed as a sign of faith.

The church was not typically American Baptist or even typically American Protestant in this way. About half the members of the church were African American and about half were European American. They had been mixed that way for many years and were proud of how open they were to each other, how much they affirmed each other's place as children of God.

Then one day a few years before either Jane or I came to the church, one of the ministers "came out." He announced that he was gay, that he was a homosexual man, and he introduced the congregation to his partner, who soon joined the church and became a member of the choir.

Frankly, it was not all that easy for many of the congregation to take, and it got more complicated as other people who were already in the church admitted that they were gay or lesbian too. The truth is, in some cases everybody already knew that, but they'd just never *talked* about it. And then, about the time we came to that congregation, the word was out and more gay and lesbian folk joined. And it wasn't always easy for longtime members, sitting right there in church next to a homosexual couple. Or taking Communion from the chair of the board of deacons, who was an openly gay man.

We lived with that the years that I was there, and when I left, like Paul, I kept in pretty close touch and wrote occasional letters to some of the members. But it was the pastor who followed me, and the laypeople who stayed on, who found the words to bring people together. I have no idea exactly what they said to each other, but I do know that week after week for many years, gay people and straight people, African American and Asian and Hispanic people, male people and female people, have been sitting next to each other in those pews and saying one prayer in one voice: "Our Father..." the prayer begins.

"Father" because of their faith in God. "*Our* Father," because of their love for one another as brothers and sisters in Christ.

Listen, I will tell you a mystery. When very different people sit together in the same church and at one time pray aloud to the same God, "Our Father...," when that happens, we have already affirmed one another; we have already welcomed one another to the household of our God.

"Listen," I think Paul would say, "what counts is not homosexuality or heterosexuality but faith working through love." Faith that binds us to God; love that binds us to one another.

### IV.

What count are the faith that binds us to God and the
love that binds us to one another.

One more thing. When Paul reminds the Galatians that God is their father, he is not just drawing on his Jewish heritage, and he's not just using typical old-fashioned, patriarchal language either. He is reminding them that God has reached out to them in Jesus Christ to make them part of God's own family. He is reminding them that they are all adopted. Listen to Paul:

"But when the fullness of time had come, God sent his Son, born of a woman, born under the law, in order to redeem those who were under the law, so that we might receive adoption as children. And because you are children, God has sent the Spirit of his Son into our hearts, crying 'Abba! [Our] Father!' So you are no longer a slave, but a child, and if a child then also an heir of God through Christ" (NRSV marg.) (Gal. 4:4–7).

It is not our birth that brings us to God, not our race or our gender or our sexuality, not one success we have ever achieved, not one goal we have ever accomplished. It is the love of God that reaches out to us and chooses us to be God's own: God's adopted sons and daughters, Christ's adopted sisters and brothers, and therefore—how can it not be?—sisters and brothers to one another too.

Think of the words we spoke together as we recognized Meredith's adoption of her new family: "O God, you have adopted all of us as your children. We give you thanks for these children and for Meredith, who has embraced these children as her own."

Here is the good news. God has embraced us as God's own.

"And because you are children, God has sent the Spirit of his Son into our hearts crying, 'Abba! Father!' So you are no longer a slave but a child, and if a child then also an heir."

Listen, what counts is not who we are but who we belong to. Our Father. Faith that binds us to God; love that binds us to each other. What counts is faith, working through love.

Amen.

## Chapter Two

# Mark and the Beginning of the Gospel

## The Beginning of the Gospel

So far as we can tell, it is Mark who gave the early church the idea of calling the gospels "Gospels." Mark begins his book, "The beginning of the gospel of Jesus the Messiah, the Son of God" (Mark 1:1 NRSV alt.). It seems highly unlikely that Mark thought that this was the name of the book he wrote, or more generally that he was naming a genre of literature. Much more likely he, like Paul before him, knew that a gospel was a good announcement, and his good announcement took the form of a story about Jesus, beginning with John the Baptist and ending with the empty tomb. The later church took Mark's claim about the content of his book (that it was an announcement of the good news of Jesus, Messiah, Son of God) and turned it into a claim that this *kind* of book was called a gospel. So three other canonical books were also called gospels, the Gospel according to Matthew, the Gospel according to Luke, and the Gospel according to John—and there are a number of "gospels" that were not included in the New Testament. Whether or not Mark thought that he was writing a "gospel," he did do something strikingly new: he announced the good news, not by focusing almost exclusively on Jesus' death and resurrection, as Paul did, but by telling the whole story of Jesus' ministry as a prelude to that death and resurrection. (No doubt many of the stories Mark records had been passed on by word of mouth before his book, but so far as we know he was the first believer to write down this full story as his way of proclaiming good news.)

It is also possible that Mark was deliberately providing the title for his book in the first phrase that he wrote down, but if so, the title of the book was not "the gospel of Jesus, Messiah, son of God," but "The Beginning of the Gospel of Jesus, Messiah, Son of God."[1] If Mark thought of his book not as the gospel, but as the beginning of the gospel, we can perhaps understand one of the oddest features of his book. As we now have it, Mark's Gospel ends in what appears to be the middle of the story of Jesus' resurrection; more than that, it ends in midparagraph; more than that, it ends in midsentence. The English translation tries to smooth over the difficulty: "So [the women] went out and fled from the tomb, for terror and amazement had seized them; and they said nothing to anyone, [because] they were afraid" (Mark 16:8). But the last word in the Greek is not "afraid"—it's that odd "because" ("for," NRSV). At the very least, the sentence structure would compel an early reader or hearer to expect some elaboration: "and. . . ." Or perhaps even more likely, a further explanation: "Because of that, and what else?" But there it is; the sentence ends with a conjunction.

Maybe, of course, Mark wrote a more complete ending which we have lost, one that sounded more like the endings of Matthew, Luke, and John. Some early Christians noticed that something was missing from the text—the appearances of the risen Jesus—and they added two different endings, each of which took material from the other Gospels to provide appearance narratives. Or maybe Mark had a fatal heart attack just before he could write the last page. Or he may have been interrupted and lost his train of thought, never getting around to completing the scroll.[2]

More likely Mark knew what he was doing. Or to put it differently, since all we know of this Mark is Mark 1:1–16:8, more likely the book we have before us makes its own kind of narrative and rhetorical sense. At the end of the book the women who have found the empty tomb are silent. The reader asks: So how do we know that Christ is risen? And the answer of course is: Because others have borne witness. Then the reader asks, And how shall others know that Christ is risen? And the answer of course is that we, the readers, the hearers, are to bear witness. This book is not the gospel, it is the beginning of the gospel, and the gospel continues wherever the good news is proclaimed and heard. It is the readers themselves who continue the gospel by believing and proclaiming.[3] (We shall see below that for the other Gospel writers the commission that Jesus gives to his disciples at the end of the story provides a major clue to the content of the good news. Here it's the young man who provides the commission—"Go, tell." But the response on the part of the characters in the story is silence; it is for the readers to respond with speech.)[4]

If we read Mark's book not as the fullness of the gospel but as its beginning, we need to see what the gospel's beginning looks like. If we read Mark's book as a commission for future preachers, not just for ordained preachers, but for all witnesses, we need to see what we preach and how we bear witness.

The first verse gives us a clue to which we return time and again. The good news is always and only news about this Jesus. And we can say two things about him: he is Messiah, that is, he is Israel's expected deliverer. And he is Son of God, that is (for Mark) he is the one who ransoms the whole world from sin. Part of the strategy and puzzle of Mark's Gospel will be to help us to understand who this Jesus is, how he is both Messiah and Son of God.[5]

Jesus is Messiah and Son of God in part because of what he himself preaches, and what he himself preaches is also called "gospel," "good news":

> Now after John was arrested, Jesus came to Galilee, proclaiming the good news of God, and saying, "The time is fulfilled, and the kingdom of God has come near; repent, and believe in the gospel." (Mark 1:14–15, NRSV marg.)

Here is what we can say about the good news on the basis of this one verse:

1. Jesus is the primary, exemplary proclaimer of this good news. (We will see more of this when Jesus becomes a model for the sower who goes out to sow, in Mark 4.)
2. This is the good news of God, in part because it is good news that comes from God, and partly because it is good news about God. Because we have already seen that this is good news about Jesus, we are invited to see that in this good news Jesus and the God who sent him are closely joined.
3. This is good news about God's kingdom, reign, rule, *basileia.* We shall soon see that this kingdom is not so much a place as an action, a declaration and establishment of sovereignty on God's part. Jesus is not only the proclaimer of God's victory, he is its front line.
4. This kingdom is at hand. The Greek verb catches that moment, that breath, just between promise and fulfillment, when the long-expected lover rings the doorbell, when the curtain that divides us from the child we have come to visit (at the hospital) is just being pulled open, when we recognize the beloved voice at the other end of the phone, before the first word is fully formed or heard. That's where we are in Mark's Gospel; that is the time where good news happens.
5. And we are to respond to this good news, this moment, this invitation. Open the door; step through the curtain; shout in joy at the sound of the familiar voice. Put away whatever threatens to mar this reunion. Answer the doorbell; trust the good news.

### The Exorcisms as Victories of God's Reign

The suggestion that we can best understand the kingdom or reign of God in Mark's Gospel as an event, an incursion, is not simply a twenty-first-century rush to metaphor. In the first chapters of the Gospel, Mark makes quite clear that Jesus' entrance into human history is part of a battle God is waging against the forces of Satan. The temptation, presented so starkly in this earliest Gospel, makes clear that the ministry begun in Jesus is a battle between the power of God's Spirit and the power of Satan (Mark 1:12–13). In his dispute with the scribes about the sources of his own authority, Jesus uses a brief parable that makes clear his own role in God's struggle for the world: "But no one can enter a strong man's house and plunder his property without first tying up the strong man; then indeed the house can be plundered" (Mark 3:27).

In the most elaborate of the several exorcism stories in Mark's Gospel, Jesus calms a man driven by demonic forces so strong that no human power can tie them down. "[The man with an unclean spirit] lived among the tombs; and no one could restrain him any more, even with a chain; for he had often been restrained with shackles and chains, but the chains he wrenched apart, and the shackles he broke in pieces; and no one had the strength to subdue him" (Mark 5:3–4).

Again the story that follows is not a metaphor or an allegory of something else. It is not Mark's attempt to talk therapeutic liberation using archaic terms, nor to declare political and economic liberation in some clever code. For Mark, and I daresay for Jesus, Satan was the enemy. God was engaged in apocalyptic warfare, and Jesus, driven by the Spirit, drove out those spirits who failed to serve God. It was a healthy reminder for me when early in my career I was writing about the metaphorical power of the exorcism stories in Mark's Gospel to be told by a friend from a very different culture that in his country my treasury of metaphorical imagery was rather a guide for pastoral care—exorcism was the way in which pastors called upon God to bind up the strong one who, left to his own devices, was always preying on the weak.

We always interpret cross-culturally, across continents and across ages, and it is never a matter of trying to bring the naïveté of the Bible into the sophistication of our postmodernity. It is rather that time as well as space can divide cultures; we do not tell the stories of our lives as Mark told the stories of the lives of those around him. Yet his stories can become typologies for our somewhat different stories, as our stories (far from being "simply the way it is") serve as typologies for others to see the world and to see God's incursion into that world.

So while the Gospel is never simply about psychology, for people like us who think in psychological categories and pray for salvation that knits our fractured souls, it is not simply a cheat to think of this story in therapeutic terms.

More than any theologian I know, Paul Tillich, trying to understand gospel in ontological categories, helped us understand gospel in psychological categories as well, or, perhaps more accurately, saw that ontological claims had psychological implications. For Tillich the demonic was not only a term for those forces that can drive a person, it was a term for those forces which had their own kind of attractive "divine" power and could only be cast out by the power of God. Recall Tillich on the demonic:

> A main characteristic of the tragic is the state of being blind.
> A main characteristic of the demonic is the state of being split. . . . A consequence of these splits, connected with the nature of the demonic, is the state of being "possessed" by the power which produces the split. The demoniacs are the possessed ones. The freedom of centeredness is removed by the demonic split. Demonic structures in the personal and communal life cannot be broken by acts of freedom and good will. They are strengthened by such acts—except when the changing power is a divine structure, that is, a structure of grace. [6]

Then look at this story. What drives this man, inhabited by a legion of demons, are forces beyond his control. They are forces that bind him to the past (all that wandering among the tombs). They are forces that turn him quite literally into his own worst enemy. They are forces that recognize and resist the holy: "What have you to do with me, Jesus, Son of the Most High God?" (Mark 5:7)

Here is how healing comes. It comes in a genuine power struggle. Healing does not come by means of cheap or easy assurance but by a recognition of how tough the battle is and how costly the victory. (Perhaps this early in the story not even Jesus knows fully the cost.) It comes with a word. One thing about the Bible from beginning to end: words count; words enact; words change the world. And healing comes just at the point of most resistance. The poor man is shouting at the top of his voice: "What have you to do with me, Jesus of Nazareth?" and a wise pastor would back off immediately, perhaps quickly slipping across the pastoral desk a card referring the visitor to a *real* psychotherapist. I have been immeasurably helped in my ministry both in parish and divinity school by the reminder of James Dittes, who may not have had this story in mind but could have when he wrote, "It is possible that resistance may be regarded as a form of awe which betrays simultaneously avoidance and attraction toward the enterprise and purposes of psychotherapy or of the church."[7]

When the villagers come out after the healing, what they find is the man who has been naked, dashing, gnashing, slashing himself, "sitting there, clothed and in his right mind" (Mark 5: 15). Of course the villagers are afraid. There is something, someone, here stronger than the strong one; an awesome battle has been won. (At the end of the story the women who have come to the empty tomb are also filled with fear. Another awesome battle won.)

Paul Tillich captures powerfully the image of the preacher as exorcist:

> Beyond this, you may have become aware of the fact that both physical and mental, individual and social, illness is a consequence of the estrangement of man's spirit from the divine Spirit. For this reason you have become ministers of the message of healing. You are not supposed to be physicians; you are not supposed to be psychotherapists; you are not supposed to become political reformers. But you are supposed to pronounce and to represent the healing and demon-conquering power implied in the message of the Christ, the message of forgiveness and of a new reality.[8]

We can make another typological leap. Readers of Scripture among the dispossessed and the marginalized remind us that not only individuals but social groups are often in thrall of forces they did not invent and that they cannot easily escape. Here, too, it is easy to adapt behavior that appears to be protective but is instead destructive. The liberating word is a word that empowers the oppressed to move out, away from the bonds of a dead past into the future God is winning for creation. The story will be told differently in different communities, but it is a valid retelling of this story, this struggle, this good news; and when the story is heard its fruits will be both sanity and fear.[9]

## Secrecy and Parable: The Hidden Kingdom

One of the first scholars to help us understand the particular perspective of Mark's Gospel was William Wrede, who in 1901 wrote a book called *The Messianic Secret*.[10] Wrede noticed how often in the Gospel Jesus instructs those who have been healed by him to keep quiet about the miracle, and he argued that this device was used for an apologetic purpose: to explain why some of those who had first known about Jesus had still not chosen to become his followers. If he was all that the tradition says he was, why was he not more widely known, more universally honored?

Later students of Mark have suggested that the messianic secret is part of an even broader device in Mark's Gospel, the use of secrecy, or mystery, or hidden revelation.[11] This motif is evident at a number of places in Mark's Gospel, but perhaps most clearly (or mysteriously) in Jesus' use of parables. We tend to think of parables as pithy illustrations used to make clear the themes of Jesus' more propositional preaching of the kingdom. Note, however, how Jesus explains his own use of parables to the disciples in this Gospel:

> When he was alone, those who were around him along with the twelve asked him about the parables. And he said to them, "To you has been given the mystery [marg.] of the kingdom of God, but for those outside, everything comes in parables, in order that

'they may indeed look, but not perceive,
and may indeed listen, but not understand;
so that they may not turn again and be forgiven.'"
(Mark 4:10–12)

Jesus quotes Isaiah 6:9–10 in order to make clear that the purpose of parables is as much to conceal as to reveal. They serve to separate the insiders, who "get" the gospel, from the outsiders, who do not.

Some of the puzzles of Markan parables remain puzzling to us (perhaps because we are still outsiders), but some of the themes seem fairly clear. The mystery to which they point is a mystery we can understand in the light of Jesus' crucifixion and resurrection, and the good news is that in the light of Jesus' crucifixion and resurrection we are allowed to see and to speak parabolically. Put most simply, we are allowed to see in metaphor and story the signs of what God is doing for the sake of the kingdom.

Look just at the parables in this section where Jesus (and Mark) introduce this puzzling understanding of parable:

Mark 4:1–9 is explained in Mark 4:14–20, and readers have long noticed that the explanation doesn't exactly fit the parable (at first the seed is the word and then it's the people who receive the word), but as a picture of God's mission in Jesus the story provides not just a puzzle but clues to help solve the puzzle.[12] According to Mark, the preaching of the word continues and flourishes despite opposition, indifference, and neglect. Because God is God, the harvest is abundant, but the path toward abundance is not easy or simple, either one.

In Mark 4:26–29 there is a kind of contrast between visible time and hidden time (mystery remains). In visible time the sower sows and sleeps and rises and goes about daily life. In invisible time, hidden time, God uses the gifts the sower brings to produce— "automatically"—the Greek says, the fruits of the harvest. We go about our daily lives of working and sleeping and eating and worshiping and raising our children and strengthening our marriages, and God takes the everyday stuff we bring and uses it as firstfruits of a kingdom of astonishing fulfillment and joy. Part of faithfulness is faithfully to keep going; part of faith-fulness is to know when to stop, harvest, rejoice.

Jesus' own ministry is like a mustard seed (see Mark 4:30–32). When Mark writes, he writes of a little-known figure from an obscure corner of the world (the secret Messiah), and yet Mark says to his readers that from this seed of Jesus' ministry a tree will blossom forth so large that all the birds of the air can shelter in its branches. Mark reminds the little churches to which he writes that their smallness is not a denial of the kingdom of God, but a sign of that kingdom, of a harvest yet to come, a tree yet to spring forth in its glory. Even in our time when Jesus is known and honored, if not followed, around the world, the life of faith can seem like small potatoes in the great garden of life. Yet planted faithfully, it remains full of promise, full of hope.

Gospel in the parables is the gift to look at the ordinary and find the extraordinary signs of God's goodness, the clues to the future God intends for all creation. Gospel in the parables is a puzzle, but it is a puzzle for which faith provides the crucial clues. Let those who have ears to hear, hear.

The parabolic reading of the world pervades the Gospel. Mir-acles, like parables, are mysteries. The disciples watch Jesus feed the five thousand, and then they help him feed the four thousand, and in his gracious activity there is a mystery they still fail to understand, as perhaps do we:

> And becoming aware of it, Jesus said to [the disciples], "Why are you talking about having no bread? Do you still not per-ceive or understand? Are your hearts hardened? Do you have eyes, and fail to see? Do you have ears, and fail to hear? [Notice the echoes of Mark 4.] And do you not remember? When I broke the five loaves for the five thousand, how many baskets full of broken pieces did you collect?" They said to him, "Twelve." "And the seven for the four thousand, how many baskets full of broken pieces did you collect?" And they said to him, "Seven." Then he said to them, "Do you not yet understand?" (Mark 8:17–21)

The reason for the injunctions to silence after the miracles may be that, left to themselves, those who hear about the miracles will misinterpret them, turning Jesus into a splendid magician rather than a hidden revelation of God's will and of the inbreaking kingdom. The reason Jesus always tells the disciples to be quiet about the crucifixion and resurrection he predicts is that these, too, are mysteries, only to be understood from inside; and we will only be invited inside after he has come out from the empty tomb. The cross itself becomes a parable: most people "reading" it see the failure of a self-deluded prophet with messianic pretensions; the centurion, seeing how Jesus dies, instantly becomes an insider: "Truly this man was God's Son!" (Mark 15:39). The empty tomb becomes the final parable, the ultimate mystery, and we are torn between the women, who run away in fear, and the young man who tells them and us that the crucified and risen one precedes us into Galilee, into a world waiting for good news.

### Following: His Cross and Ours

More clearly in Mark's Gospel than in any of the others, the good news of Jesus, Messiah, Son of God, is the news of the cross. Martin Kähler wrote that the Gospels were passion narratives with lengthy prologues, and at the very least we can say that Mark's Gospel drives the story from the beginning toward its climax on Golgotha.[13] In Mark 3:6, with Jesus' ministry just under way: "The Pharisees went out and immediately conspired with the Herodians against him, how to destroy him." At the central, climactic moment of this Gospel, which tries to show us who Jesus is, Peter speaks the confession, "You are the Christ," and Jesus tells him what that title has to mean:

> Then he began to teach them that the Son of Man must undergo great suffering, and be rejected by the elders, the chief priests, and the scribes, and be killed, and after three days rise again. (Mark 8:31)

This is the first of three times that Jesus explicitly predicts his own suffering, death, and resurrection. The last parable, the last mystery Jesus discloses to the disciples, is the parable of the vineyard owner who sends his beloved son, whom the tenants of the vineyard seize, kill, and cast out of the vineyard itself (Mark 12:1–11).

At the beginning of his story, Mark has told us that this Jesus is both Messiah (Christ) and Son of God. As the story proceeds, God's own voice twice declares Jesus God's Son (1:11; 9:7). Demons, who are spiritual forces able to understand spiritual truths, also declare that Jesus is God's Son (see Mark 3:11, similarly 1:24; 5:7). But the first and only human to make the essential confession of Jesus' sonship is the Roman centurion at the climactic moment of the story.

> When it was noon, darkness came over the whole land until three in the afternoon. At three o'clock Jesus cried out with a loud voice, "Eloi, Eloi, lema sabachthani?" which means, "My God, my God, why have you forsaken me?" When some of the bystanders heard it, they said, "Listen, he is calling for Elijah." And someone ran, filled a sponge with sour wine, put it on a stick, and gave it to him to drink, saying, "Wait, let us see whether Elijah will come to take him down." Then Jesus gave a loud cry and breathed his last. And the curtain of the temple was torn in two, from top to bottom. Now when the centurion, who stood facing him, saw that in this way he breathed his last, he said, "Truly this man was God's Son!" (Mark 15:33–39)

Here, as in Matthew, the death is almost unbearably stark. There is no pious commendation of Christ's spirit into God's hands, as in Luke, and no cry of triumphant return, as in John. The cry is a cry of dereliction, abandonment. Readers puzzle about how to read this climax of the story, this penultimate mystery or parable. What is it that the centurion, now become a paradigmatic insider, sees?

Some have thought that the centurion, or the reader for whom the centurion stands surrogate, realizes that Jesus here quotes Psalm 22:1. Because the conclusion of the psalm is far more hopeful than its beginning, readers have hoped that Mark is reminding us both of the desolation and of the promise. The turning point of the psalm comes with verse 21b, "from the horns of the wild oxen you have rescued me," and moves on to an assurance of God's triumphant power over nations and history.

Susan Garrett writes thoughtfully of the way in which the cross becomes the final test of Jesus' faithfulness, a test that begins in the wilderness with Satan and ends here in this final proof of devotion and loyalty to God. Jesus' sonship is attested by his faithfulness, and this is what the centurion sees:

"By standing fast, by refusing to be led astray even in this most severe test of affliction, Jesus shows himself to be truly the Son of God, one who is 'tried and true' and worthy to offer himself as a sacrificial burnt offering to God. God accepts Jesus' self-offering as sufficient to atone for sin."[14]

Others, myself included, see in this text above all another riddle, puzzle, paradox. Jesus can cry out to God from his sense of abandonment, but still cries "*My* God." He doubts God in the presence of God.[15] His sense of abandonment is unfathomable precisely because the one who has deserted him is not only the sovereign God, maker of heaven and earth, but his own father. It is not so much that in the cross God sacrifices God's Son for the sake of humankind, but that in Jesus' sacrifice on the cross God knows the suffering that lies at the heart of humankind.

André Trocmé was the pastor of the Huguenot church in the village of Le Chambon in occupied France, during World War II. During the war he and his wife and family and the other staff and congregation of the church helped numbers of Jews to escape the Nazi terror. Toward the end of the war Trocmé had to face his own terror, when his beloved son Jean Pierre, either by accident or choice, was hanged. Trocmé later wrote of this:

Even today I carry a death within myself, the death of my son, and I am like a decapitated pine. Pine trees do not regenerate their tops. They stay twisted, crippled. They grow in thickness, perhaps, and that is what I am doing. . . . Under a scar that the years have thickened little by little, there bleeds in the depths of my being an incurable wound.[16]

More than any of the other Gospels, Mark's Gospel shows us how the crucifixion wounded God; how in Jesus Christ the suffering of God joins the suffering of humankind; how from now until all eternity God bears in God's heart that suffering and loss, like a scar, like a tree.

If the great puzzle of Mark's Gospel is that Christ's death is the sign of Christ's sonship and God's love, the smaller puzzle is like unto it, human life is most alive when we, too, follow in the way of the cross.

After Peter makes the great, climactic confession that Jesus is the Messiah and Jesus tells the disciples that his messiahship will require suffering and death, Peter vehemently protests. We can suspect that Peter protests not only for Jesus' sake, but for his own, because almost immediately Jesus makes clear that the way of the Messiah foreshadows the way of those who would follow him: "If any want to become my followers, let them deny themselves and take up their cross and follow me. For those who want to save their life will lose it, and those who lose their life for my sake, and for the sake of the gospel, will save it" (Mark 8:34–35).[17]

When James and John ask Jesus if they can sit beside him in his coming glory, he warns them of the meaning of what they ask: "You do not know what you are asking. Are you able to drink the cup that I drink, or be baptized with the baptism that I am baptized with?" (Mark 10:38). The sacraments to which he calls them are the sacraments of obedient suffering and death.

At the end of the Gospel (16:6), when the young man proclaims the good news to the women, he tells them that the one who has been crucified is the one who is risen, but equally he tells them that the risen one, the victorious one, is still the one who has been crucified, who bears his wounds for eternity. When the same young man says to remind the disciples that Jesus "is going ahead" of them, we can be sure that the way on which he leads them will include suffering, sacrifice, loss.

Frederick Buechner's saint, Godric, has a kind of motto that captures the shape of Mark's Gospel: "All's lost; all's found."[18] Perhaps the greatest challenge of Mark's good news in a time and a nation where so many of us have so much is that we learn that life is found not in the getting but in the giving up; that the way to gain lies through loss, and the way to life lies through death. The demand for sacrifice is the invitation to blessing. This is odd good news, but good news all the same.

### The Kingdom to Come

While many commentators have seen the passion narrative as the key to the themes and purpose of Mark's Gospel, others have seen the key to be its strong belief that Jesus will soon return and establish the kingdom in its fullness. The parable of the mustard seed (4:30–32) is not just a metaphor for the contrast between Jesus' small ministry and its great fruits in history. It is a promise of that kingdom that stands at the door when he first preaches the gospel but which at the end of time will consume human history in all its fullness.

By this reading, Mark 13 is not just an unfortunate holdover from the Jewish apocalypticism of the first century; it is the heart of what Mark's Jesus has to declare, the heart of the good news.

Rudolf Bultmann is famous for his project of demythologizing the New Testament, but in some ways his larger project was to de-apocalypticize the gospel message. Drawing on clues in Paul's letters and the Fourth Gospel, he tried to do this by transforming eschatological hope from a cosmic to a personal promise. And he tried to do this by translating the eschatological future into the future of authentic existence, which the believer can choose in any given moment. Eschatology was no longer future and cosmic, it was present and personal, especially in proclamation:

> It is the paradox of the Christian message that the eschato-
> logical event, according to Paul and John, is not to be under-
> stood as a dramatic cosmic catastrophe but as happening
> within history, beginning with the appearance of Jesus Christ
> and in continuity with this occurring again and again in his-
> tory, but not as the kind of historical development which can
> be confirmed by the historian. It becomes an event repeat-
> edly in preaching and faith. Jesus Christ is the eschatologi-
> cal event not as an established fact of past time but as
> repeatedly present, as addressing you and me here and now
> in preaching.[19]

While we may not be persuaded by Bultmann's solution to the
problem of apocalyptic eschatology, it is impossible to deny that
it is a problem. At eucharistic services at the school where I teach,
at any rate, it is impossible not to note a kind of falling off in conviction when the congregation moves through the great affirma-
tion: "Christ has died; Christ is risen; Christ will come again."

Our problem is at least twofold. First, there seems no doubt
that for Mark as for much of early Christianity the belief in Jesus'
second coming and in the redemption of history was not a belief
in some far-distant event. Mark and his community expected that
consummation to be just around the corner, or to use our earlier
metaphor, at the threshold, ready to break in: "And [Jesus] said to
them, 'Truly I tell you, there are some standing here who will not
taste death until they see that the kingdom of God has come with
power" (Mark 9:1;[20] see also Mark 13:30).

Second, the scenario that Mark presupposes for the consummation of history is simply too geocentric and perhaps too
anthropocentric for our understanding of cosmos and therefore
of the cosmos's Creator. In his novel *The City of God*, E. L. Doctorow suggests the ways in which our vision of God, and therefore of God's providence, needs to be reshaped in the light of what
we know about the universe. A Nobel laureate in physics named
Murray Seligman gets up to speak in a kind of open forum at his
local synagogue:

The Hebrews conceived of a cosmic God, a magnificent single God of the universe, but naturally in terms of their land and its crops and its tribal wars, and His up and down relationship with them. So He was localized to a great degree, the Creator, the applicable honorifics being Lord and King. All very understandable. . . .

. . . But if you take the trouble to think of what we know today about the universe, about how it is roughly fifteen billion years old, and how it suddenly inflated and has been expanding since, how space is ineluctably time, and time is ineluctably space . . . and how the universe in its perhaps ever increasing rate of expansion accommodates not just galaxies, which contain millions of stars, but multiple clusters of galaxies that are themselves strung out in clusters of clusters . . . and with all of this a dark matter we are yet to understand . . . the Creator, blessed be His name, who can make solid reality or what we perceive as reality out of indeterminate, unpredictable wave/particle functions . . . that all of this from Himself or Herself or Itself, who is by definition vaster and greater than all this . . . Well, I am forced to ask the traditionalists among us if our Creator, or blessed name, is perhaps not insufficiently praised by our usage of the honorifics Lord and King, let alone Father and Shepherd.[21]

Complicated, and far beyond my ken, is the realization that space and time are not separate realities unaffected by one another: Our sense of the future and our sense of the expansiveness of the cosmos play off against each other in such a way that it is impossible simply to think about a future event where a God exclusively focused on our planet brings an end to local time.

Mark 13 itself is both apocalyptic and more than apocalyptic, both affirming and critical of particular expectations for God's future. For one thing, it contains a clear warning against the kind of checking of signs that tries to work out an elaborate timetable for what will finally be beyond time: "But about that day or hour no one knows, neither the angels in heaven, nor the Son, but only the Father" (Mark 13:32).[22] For another thing, the references to signs and portents in the first part of the chapter are somewhat qualified by the more typical Markan move to parable at the end of the chapter: "From the fig tree learn its lesson. . . ." (13:28) "It is like a man going on a journey. . . ." (13:34). The future is God's future, but it is better read through metaphor than through calculation; right expectation is more like poetry than like algebra.

Nonetheless, Jesus in Mark's Gospel does not sound like Bultmann, or much like Bultmann's favorite evangelist, John. What Bultmann seeks to relativize, Mark's Gospel most affirms. Bultmann tends to understand eschatology as focused on the individual and focused in the present. For Mark eschatology is quite different:

The *future* of all creation is in God's hands and will show forth God's purpose.

The future of *all creation* is in God's hands and will show forth God's purpose.

I have been helped in thinking eschatologically by seeking to move outside my own comfortable social location to think with those who, like many of Jesus' hearers and Mark's, lived under persecution, danger, threat, and for whom this world provided very little comfort indeed. Ched Myers helps:

> By Mark's era [apocalyptic] was well established as a discourse of political protest. According to [Richard] Horsley, the social function of apocalyptic was to fire the socio-political imagination of the oppressed. First, in renewing old symbols and reappropriating Hebrew narratives of liberation, it functions as "remembering." Secondly, it promoted a "creative revisioning" of a future in which God restored justice and full humanity to all. And thirdly, the dualistic combat myth functioned as a *"critical demystifying* of the pretensions and practices of the established order."[23]

I return as I so often do to St. Paul and to his word to the Corinthian church which affirms the faith we also see portrayed in Mark's Gospel: "If for this life only we have hoped in Christ, we are of all people most to be pitied" (1 Cor. 15:19).

## Irony and Resurrection

Though the devil is a great ironist,
so is the Lord.[24]

Numbers of commentators have noticed how much Mark's Gospel depends on irony. For many of us Wayne Booth has been the guide to the function of irony in literature, and Robert Fowler the guide to irony in Mark.[25]

The success of irony depends on the reader or hearer knowing what the actor does not know. Sometimes we discover dramatic irony. An incident means more or means differently than it appears to mean. We read Lincoln's words from the Gettysburg address: "The world will little note nor long remember what we have said here." And because we know what he could not have known, that schoolchildren for six score and seven years have been memorizing his speech, we hear his claim ironically.

Sometimes we find verbal irony. A statement means more or means other than it appears to mean. A statement intended sarcastically turns out to be true literally. In the movie *Young Einstein*, for example, the hero's teacher throws up his hands in disgust after young Albert botches yet another simple math problem, and asks, "You're pretty smart, aren't you?"

Successful irony depends on our knowing better than the characters know. One device that makes this possible is "reliable commentary."[26] In Mark both the narrator and God are reliable commentors, and Jesus soon proves to be reliable as well. From the reliable narrator we immediately get the information that will help us understand the irony of the rest of the Gospel: "The beginning of the good news of Jesus Christ the Son of God." That is, in Mark's Gospel it is not just that nothing is what it seems, but that we have clues to the divine reality that undercuts the obvious appearances on which people too easily rely.

The passion narrative in Mark is especially rich in irony, an irony that is permeated with gospel. Perhaps the quickest definition of gospel irony is that through gospel irony we know that what appears to be bad news is good news.

In a moment of dramatic irony the soldiers cry to Jesus, "Prophesy!" (Mark 14:65). They think they are being sarcastic, but in fact Jesus has already prophesied this very moment (in Mark 10:34), and in the next scene, Peter will deny Jesus three times, just as Jesus has also prophesied.

The passion narrative is full of verbal irony. The chief priests look at Jesus on the cross and taunt him: "He saved others; he cannot save himself. Let the Messiah, the King of Israel, come down from the cross now, so that we may see and believe" (Mark 15:31–32). With our distance from the scene and from our perspective of faith, we know that what they think to be bad news is good news. Precisely because Jesus refuses to save himself, he is able to save others. And we know that the requirement of faith is just the opposite of what the high priests think: true belief is belief in Jesus on the cross, the belief that the centurion will show in Mark 15:39.

For Mark, gospel is a kind of double vision; the faithful can understand what the world sees when it looks at Jesus, but we see something not only different but precisely opposite. Clifton Black's reading of Mark in comparison with 1 Corinthians 1 notes the irony: "But we proclaim Christ crucified, a stumbling block to Jews and foolishness to Gentiles, but to those who are the called, both Jews and Greeks, Christ the power of God and the wisdom of God. For God's foolishness is wiser than human wisdom, and God's weakness is stronger than human strength" (1 Cor. 1:23–25).[27]

The presentation of the disciples in Mark's Gospel is also ironic. Jesus speaks to them in the midst of his discourse on the parables: "To you has been given the mystery [marg.] of the kingdom of God, but for those outside everything comes in parables, in order that 'they may indeed look, but not perceive'" (Mark 4:11–12). Yet time and again it is these supposed insiders who don't get the parables, or the passion predictions either (see, for instance, Mark 8:17–18, Mark 8:33, Mark 10:35–40), and apparent "outsiders," who do understand what faith requires, see what faith sees, looking they see and hearing they understand. So the Syrophoenician woman knows better than the disciples, perhaps better than Jesus, the extent of his authority. The nameless father knows what the disciples never understand, that by bringing to Jesus both his faith and his lack of faith he brings enough for the miracle of healing. The anonymous centurion sees what neither the insiders of Israel nor the insiders of Jesus' own circle have yet discerned: surely this was the Son of God. Irony is a world where apparently bad news is good news and apparent outsiders turn out to be at the very center of the circle.

Thus resurrection is the final irony. What appears to be the case is precisely not the case; in the most astonishing reversal the tomb is empty and the crucified one is the risen one. In his parable Jesus gives the ironic reading of his own future: "The stone which the builders rejected has [ironically] become the cornerstone." And then the explanation of the irony: "This was the Lord's doing, and it is amazing in our eyes" (Mark 12:10–11).

At the empty tomb, are the women insiders or outsiders? Are those of us who hear the story or read it insiders or outsiders? Do we know what fullness this apparent emptiness promises? Does this stone, set aside, remind us of the stone the builders set aside, only to become the cornerstone of God's new temple, God's new kingdom? Those who have eyes to see, let them see. Then let them tell others what the faithful can see. The beginning of the good news.

Patrick Henry has written a helpful book of reflections and memoirs called *The Ironic Christian's Companion* in which he writes, "An ironic Christian inhabits a world that is more 'as if' than 'just like,' a world fashioned by a God of surprises. The grace of this God is mysterious, sneaky."[28] Mark's Gospel provides texts aplenty for those of us who sometimes need to see the world ironically. Our very distance from the obvious may be the distance in which God makes God's own self known. Things are not always what they appear to be. How ironic. Good news.

*Sermon*

# The Beginning of the Gospel

## MARK 1:1–14

I'll bet you've noticed in *Time* and *Newsweek* and even on public television how much interest there is in the historical Jesus. Who was Jesus?
What can we know about where he lived and what he did and his family and his teachings? What's accurate in the Bible and what's less than
accurate? And what do we learn by learning about other religious figures and movements of his time—about the rabbis, say, or the Greek
philosophers, or the people who wrote the Dead Sea Scrolls?

These are interesting questions, but they are not the question that the
Gospel writers were worried about. Maybe because it hadn't been so
long since Jesus was among them, or maybe because they weren't as
sophisticated historically as we are, they didn't ask much about the historical Jesus, about evidence and written accounts and the relationship
to other religious figures of his time.

And maybe there is another reason why they weren't so interested in
who Jesus was. It was because they were convinced that Jesus was still alive
and active among them. What they wanted to know was not: "Who was
he?" but "Who is he?" Not, "What did he do?" but "What is he doing?"

One way to answer that question, "What is he doing?" was to tell
stories about him. The stories were not just stories about what Jesus
used to mean, they were stories about what he still meant—in their lives
and now, by extension, in our lives too. And that brings us to the evangelist, the writer, we call Mark.

### I.

As far as we know, Mark did something that had never been done
before. He wrote a gospel. Oh, people had preached *the* gospel for

Preached at First United Methodist Church, Wichita Falls, Texas, during Lent
1998.

years before Mark came along. Peter had preached the gospel, and Paul had preached the gospel and written about the gospel, and so undoubtedly had many other men and women, some of whose names we know and some of whom are known only to God. The gospel was the good news. The good news, as Paul puts it in one of his most famous passages, that in Christ God was reconciling the world to God's own self. The good news was that God had sent Jesus who brought us to God, or who brought God to us. That was the good news; that was the gospel.

As far as we know, Mark is the first person to decide to preach the gospel by writing *a* gospel. "How may I present the good news to the people in my community?" he asked himself. He knew that the good news had to be the news that Christ had died and risen again for the sake of the world. But he also decided that for this news to be good enough, people needed to know who this Jesus was who died and rose again—what his life meant for his first disciples, and what it might mean for disciples ever after.

So Mark told the story of Jesus' dying and rising again, but before he got to that story he told a good deal about Jesus. About Jesus speaking in parables. About Jesus healing the sick. About Jesus casting out demons—and money changers. About Jesus arguing with religious and political leaders. About Jesus making some people angry and other people indescribably glad.

## II.

When he had finished writing his book, Mark put a title on the book. Here is what the title said: "The Beginning of the Gospel of Jesus the Christ, the Son of God." Mark didn't know that people would call his book a gospel. He just thought his book was a good way of preaching *the* gospel. Just as Peter and Paul had preached the gospel and Paul had written letters about the gospel, Mark had written this story of Jesus' ministry, followed by his death, followed by his resurrection. Mark knew that it was the gospel, but he didn't know that we would also call it a gospel.

And something else. When Mark wrote that title, "The Beginning of the Gospel of Jesus the Christ, the Son of God," I think that was the title of the whole book, not just an introduction to the first chapter. The whole book wasn't called "The Gospel of Jesus the Christ, the Son of God." The whole book was called "The Beginning of the Gospel of Jesus the Christ, the Son of God." Because the good news of Jesus Christ the Son of God doesn't end with his crucifixion, and the good news of Jesus Christ the Son of God does not even end with his resurrection. The good news of Jesus Christ the Son of God goes on, continues, wherever people follow him and proclaim him and sing hymns about him and even listen to sermons about him.

Mark 1:1–16:8 is not the good news about Jesus Christ. It is the beginning of that good news. Further the Gospel ends in the middle of a sentence, a stylistic way of reminding us that the Gospel isn't finished. It is as if when I get to the end of this morning's sermon, instead of saying, "Amen," I say, "Because . . .," and then say, "Let's sing a hymn." You'd say, "That sermon never quite got finished." Well, Mark's Gospel ends "because . . .," and it never quite got finished, because we still live in that Gospel in our own lives. Till kingdom come. Literally, till kingdom come.

### III.

Of course even beginnings have to have a beginning. If the whole book is the beginning of the gospel, Mark 1:1–14 is the beginning of the book. And I want us to notice how the beginning begins. It begins with the Old Testament. The very first words, "The beginning," remind us of the very first words of the Old Testament, "In the beginning." And as soon as the title of the book is written, the first voice we hear is the voice of an Old Testament prophet, Isaiah:

> As it is written in the book of the prophet Isaiah,
> "See, I am sending my messenger ahead of you,
>     who will prepare your way;
> the voice of one crying out in the wilderness:
>     'Prepare the way of the Lord,
>     make his paths straight.'"

For Mark the good news begins with what we call the Old Testament, what our Jewish neighbors call Tanakh, and what for Jesus and the disciples was just plain Scripture. And the truth is, though we remember best the shepherds and the wise men, every one of our Gospels can only get under way by calling attention to the Old Testament, because the truth is we can't get to the good news of Jesus in any other way.

In Luke's Gospel, even before the shepherds bow, there are songs sung by Mary and by Zechariah that sound just like Old Testament psalms; and the very first words Jesus speaks are words from this same prophet, Isaiah. In Matthew's Gospel, before we get to the birth or the magi we go through the genealogy that fixes Jesus firmly in the history of Abraham and David and Rahab and Ruth. And in the first verse of John's Gospel, "In the beginning was the Word,"we hear the first verse of the Hebrew Bible, Genesis 1:1, "In the beginning . . . God." It's hard enough to know what John is saying in this astonishing prologue, but if we don't know Genesis, we haven't got a clue.

Some years ago I was on the search committee looking for a new chaplain of Yale University. One of the members of the search committee was a distinguished Jewish psychiatrist, Donald Cohen. One of the responsibilities of the committee was to travel to various churches to hear candidates preach on their home turf. Donald said that as a Jew the one thing that amazed him was how much Christian worship talked about the Jews. Jews can go to synagogue week after week and not have to talk much at all about Christians, but Christians can't get through a worship service without Israel, the prophets, the law, the promises.

Sometimes Christians worry about Judaism in ways that are wise and open, and sometimes in ways that are foolish and closed, but Donald had it right. Part of the Christian deal is that we can only understand ourselves in the light of God's dealings with Israel, and we can only understand Jesus as the Jew he was. There is no way to him that does not go through Abraham and Sarah and Moses and Miriam and the psalms and the prophets. They are his family, and if we would be his brothers and sisters, we pray God to be adopted into that family too.

The beginning of the beginning of the gospel of Jesus Christ is Isaiah and Genesis and the Psalms. Thanks be to God.

## IV.

For Mark the beginning of the good news also begins with John the Baptist. John—the prophet in the wilderness—is so much less appealing than the babe in the manger. Not swaddling clothes, but camel's hair and a leather belt. And worse yet, John the Baptist preaches not peace on earth and goodwill among people, but "a baptism of repentance for the forgiveness of sins." The good news is also tough news. There is no way to get to Jesus without going through John the Baptist. There is no end run around the demanding prophet to get to the redeeming Christ.

And again Mark is not so quirky as might first appear. Luke has the angels and the shepherds; Matthew has the magi; John has the prologue and the Word made flesh—but in all four Gospels before the grown-up Jesus can give one sermon or do one miracle, there is John the Baptist. There is no way to Jesus that doesn't go through the Old Testament, and there is no way to Jesus that does not stop and listen to John.

What John preaches, of course, is baptism of repentance for the forgiveness of sins. The heart of the matter is repentance. The good news of the gospel begins with repenting of the bad news of our lives before the gospel came along. And John the Baptist stands as the stark reminder that Jesus' arrival isn't just a matter of giving, it's a matter of giving up. Letting go whatever that old life is that keeps you from receiving the new life that comes with the incarnation of Christ our Lord.

Perhaps more than any novelist of the twentieth century, Graham Greene puzzled about sin and repentance and redemption. In one of his early novels, *The End of the Affair*, Greene tells the story of a woman named Sarah, who is married to Henry but in love with Maurice. Her affair with Maurice is full of passion and delight and deceit and regret. More and more she is nagged by a vision of some fuller life that includes not only fidelity to her husband, but fidelity to a God in whom she barely believes.

It is World War II; it's London. Sarah is in the hotel room waiting for Maurice. She hears the air-raid sirens and a terrible explosion. Sarah is sure that Maurice is dead.

These are her words:

I knelt down on the floor; I was mad to do such a thing; I never even had to do it as a child—my parents never believed in prayer, any more than I do. I hadn't any idea what to say. Maurice was dead. Extinct. There wasn't such a thing as a soul. . . . I knelt and put my head on the bed and wished I could believe. Dear God, I said—why dear, why dear?—make me believe. I can't believe. Make me, I said, I'm . . . a fake, and I hate myself. I can't do anything of myself. *Make* me believe. I shut my eyes tight . . . and I said, I will believe. Let him be alive, and I *will* believe. Give him a chance. Let him have his happiness. That wasn't enough. It doesn't hurt to believe. So I said, I love him and I'll do anything if You'll make him alive. I said very slowly, I'll give him up forever, only let him be alive . . . and I said, people can love without seeing each other can't they; they love You all their lives without seeing You, and then he came in the door, and he was alive, and I thought, now the agony of being without him starts.[29]

The agony of being without him, the surprising possibilities of being with God, a return to her husband, the beginnings of faith. This is the beginning of gospel, dear friends, but it is not just a matter of smiling faces and cheerful songs. The way to Jesus is sometimes a hard way. The way to Jesus leads through John the Baptist and the repentance of sins. That is tough news. It is good news too.

## V.

You could fairly say that for Mark the Gospel begins with Lent and not with Advent at all. It begins with John the Baptist and the hard demand to repent—the difficult demand to give up.

"What are you giving up for Lent?" we ask in our more devout modes and moods. Chocolate, maybe. The movies, maybe. Or we ourselves think of those little things we'll give up, only to pick them up again blessedly at Eastertide, just in time for chocolate eggs and before the summer blockbuster movies get their sneak previews at the local theater.

The Lent to which Mark's Gospel calls is a Lent of the soul, and what we give up now we shall not take up again in forty days. Mark's Lent is not about putting aside; it is about putting away. Not about temporary inconvenience, but about life-changing repentance. John the Baptizer, that scraggy, uncouth prophet, stands as a constant reminder that the good news begins with hard news.

> Maybe this Lent we should lay down that old jealousy that has poisoned a relationship and soured our own joy. Maybe we should lay that down.
> That old regret that we didn't go the other direction, all those years ago; time to lay it down.
> The disappointment in someone we loved; the disappointment in ourselves; lay it down.
> The anger at those who did not value us as we deserved; lay it down.
> You know what it is, that damned thing that you carry that can turn even the good news of Jesus Christ into the same old blah. Lay it down.

Lent is repentance time. You can bring it all. You can put it down. You can leave it with the Christ, who is strong enough to bear it all.

It's new beginning time.

Good news.

## Chapter Three

# Matthew: The Gospel of the Kingdom

## Gospel as Good News of the Kingdom

R eaders of this book may remember that early in my ministry, James Gustafson, the distinguished Christian ethicist and theologian, who was not only my colleague and friend, but was also a parishioner of the church where I served, accused me of a preacher's devotion to St. Paul so monogamous as to be mono-maniacal. He claimed that I had left other biblical strains, not only out of my affection, but out of my view. And the biblical treasure he cited as most conspicuously absent from my homiletical storehouse was the Gospel of Matthew.

Ulrich Luz taught New Testament for many years at the University of Berne and has written the most comprehensive and helpful commentary on Matthew's Gospel that I know. An insight from Luz about the Gospel of Matthew informs everything I want to say about this Gospel and the ways in which it can become good news for us. Luz notices a feature of Matthew's editing. Assuming that Matthew draws heavily on Mark's Gospel for his own work, when Matthew comes to Jesus' opening sermon in Mark, he interprets it in his own way:

In Mark, Jesus says: "The time is fulfilled, and the kingdom of God is at hand [NRSV marg.], repent, and believe in the gospel [marg.]" (Mark 1:15). In Matthew, at the same point, the opening of his ministry, Jesus says: "Repent, for the kingdom of heaven has come near" (Matt. 4:17). Now, says Luz, Matthew knows perfectly well that what Jesus preaches when he begins to preach is gospel. What Matthew wants to underline is that gospel *is* precisely what Jesus has to say about the kingdom of heaven. Luz says:

> Gospel is for the evangelist nothing else than the kingdom proclamation of the earthly Jesus and not a Christological kerygma which can be separated from it. . . . It becomes clear in an exemplary way that in Jesus' proclamation according to Matthew the imperative precedes and dominates.[1]

In like manner also, when Matthew does refer to the gospel, to the good news, it is to the good news of the kingdom that he refers.

> The proclamation of the Kingdom is itself good news:
> It is good news that the reign of God is near. (It is good news that anyone reigns at all; that was no more self-evident in the first century than in the twenty-first.)
> It is good news that the one who reigns is God.
> It is good news that we are invited, called, even commanded to be disciples of the God who reigns.

We can begin by noting the ways in which the imperative demands of the kingdom can themselves provide good news; the ways in which—perhaps astonishingly—law is also gospel. The demands of the Torah, the new Torah, are themselves good news. The Sermon on the Mount is the summary of the New Torah for life in the kingdom. It is full of strong imperatives and strenuous demands: the demands themselves can be good news.

*The demands of the kingdom are good news because they validate the significance of our lives.* I think this is part of what Calvin implies when he reflects on the beginning of the Sermon on the Mount. "There is only one consolation by which the sharpness of the cross [we bear] and all other evils are mitigated, even made sweet, and that is for us to be assured that we have blessing in the very midst of our miseries, for our endurance is blessed by the Lord, and a happier outcome will ensue."[2]

I recall an incident very early in my preaching career. I returned to the church of my youth to preach, and preached on a favorite text, the prodigal son. The point of the sermon was not so much the return of the prodigal or the joy of the father but the recalcitrance of the elder brother, who (at least at story's end) still refuses to recognize the abundant grace of the loving father and join in the celebration of his brother's return. In appropriate, fresh-out-of-divinity-school fashion, I berated the brother as a self-righteous prig because he somehow thought that his own unwavering fidelity should commend him to his father.

After church I was taken to dinner by a pillar of the church, a trustee of long standing and an upstanding citizen, husband, and father. "I always think the elder brother gets a raw deal," he said. Then, knowingly or unknowingly, my friend moved from Luke to Matthew. "I have given my life to trying to be a good member of my community, my family, and my church, and at the end I don't want Christ to say, 'Why were you so self-righteous?' I want him to say: 'Well done, thou good and faithful servant.'"(See Matt. 25:21 RSV.)

Here is one way of understanding the good news in Matthew. What we do matters because who we are matters. If our doing good is not good and our doing bad not genuinely bad, if there is neither judgment nor commendation, then grace itself is thin and wasted.

William Muehl, who taught preaching at Yale for many years, was, I think, the faculty member who most hated Tillich's sermon "You Are Accepted," and in his Beecher lectures (as in his sermons) he provided a Matthean reading of the good news:

> I am not suggesting that most Christians do whatever good works they do out of fear that they will be struck down by a bolt of lightning, if they fail to do good works. I am suggesting that they are very often prompted in part by the conviction that God expects something of them—that in some mysterious way which they do not understand, their lives

will be better, if they make some honest effort to meet that expectation. No amount of passionate reiteration of the word of unmerited grace will shake that conviction, not because people want to live in fear of God, but because they need to believe that there is form and meaning in their daily lives. And they sense that meaning must be earned, that even God cannot give meaning as a gift.[3]

We can put it differently. The parable of the prodigal son has both its Pauline moment and its Matthean moment. In the Pauline moment, the penitent son is welcomed by the father running down the road to greet him. In the Matthean moment the elder brother is encouraged by the father heading out from the house to invite him in. Note what the (Matthean) father in the Lukan parable does not say. He does not say: "You self-righteous prig, how dare you trust in your own merits." He says, "Son, you are always with me, and all that is mine is yours" (Luke 15:31). It sounds a good deal like Matthew. "Well done, thou good and faithful servant." (And of course the next invitation to come to the party is a very Lukan read of the Matthean "Enter into the joy of your master," with the reminder that the father's joy has room for the penitent sinner and for the faithful servant, both.) (See Matt. 25:21, author's trans.)

The imperative, too, provides a kind of good news. It is good news that we are allowed, invited, commanded to serve the sovereign Lord. It is good news that we are invited to be servants of the King and of the kingdom. It is good news that we are called to be responsible.

Does our righteousness earn the righteousness of God? Or does our righteousness respond to God's righteousness? Those are our questions more than Matthew's questions. God does right and invites us to do what is right as well. God's invitations often look like commands; that is the privilege of sovereignty. But that the very God should command *us*—that is astonishing good news.[4]

Let me put this another way. In chapter 1, we noted that in

Galatians Paul is concerned with the ability of markers, especially the markers of diet and circumcision, to separate Christians one from another. In Matthew's Gospel there is also a concern with markers, but these markers work quite differently. *They are themselves good news.*

First, for Matthew, markers help Christians separate themselves from the worlds in which they live, primarily the world of the synagogue. In that sense markers help make a new Christian world, and instead of destroying community, as they threaten to do in Galatians, markers build community.

I am convinced by scholars who argue that in Matthew's Gospel the separation between church and synagogue, between, say, Sabbath-keeping Jews and Sunday-worshiping Jews, is still a vivid memory if not a present crisis.[5]

Matthew's concern is that the new community find the rules that separate it more clearly from the synagogue but that also bind Christians to one another. Christian leaders act as new scribes (Matt. 13:52). Christian community succeeds the binding and loosing of the synagogue community (Matt. 18:18–22). And Christian righteousness exceeds that of those who have been left behind. Note the instances:

> When you give, don't give like the hypocrites. (Matt. 6:2)
> When you pray, don't pray like the hypocrites. (Matt. 6:5)
> When you fast, don't wear long faces like the hypocrites.
>    (Matt. 6:16)

The new identity is defined in part by being successor to the old, and in part by being different from the old. The new righteousness is still righteousness, but richer than the righteousness that went before.

Second, the markers are more than markers; they are signposts that provide guidance along the way. Here I suppose one can rightly say that Matthew's understanding of righteousness is in some ways less radical than Paul's, less trusting of a version of

Christian freedom. While it is clear that Paul has all kinds of suggestions for the life of Christian faith, he seems less clear what principles, what laws, might be irrevocable and permanently binding.

While few have entirely accepted Benjamin Bacon's suggestion that Matthew's Gospel represents a revised Torah, with the five books of the Pentateuch echoed in the five great sermons of Matthew, there is no question that Jesus does represent a new Moses.[6] As the first Moses on Sinai presented the laws that would guide Israel on its journey to the promised land, so Jesus, the second Moses, in the Sermon on the Mount presents the laws that will guide the church on its journey toward the fullness of the kingdom.

> Enter through the narrow gate; for the gate is wide and the road is easy that leads to destruction, and there are many who take it. For the gate is narrow and the road is hard that leads to life, and there are few who find it. (Matt. 7:13–14)

Put another way: In a Matthean community when we pray the petition of the Lord's Prayer, "Your will be done," we do not simply have to guess what that will look like; nor do we have to wonder what our responsibility is in living out that will.

We can surely say too that for Matthew the demands of the new Torah, the markers, are good news because they build the Christian community, which is the foreshadowing or the outpost of the kingdom. Christian community is marked by its difference from the old world around it; Christian community is marked by the guideposts that show the way for a common pilgrimage.

Matthew's Gospel is the church's gospel, not just because the church has always loved it but because Matthew loves the church. The kingdom is breaking in, and in the meantime this community of people forgive one another, feed one another, discipline one another, and pray with one another.

Stanley Hauerwas and William Willimon tell us that as

church we are aliens and strangers in an indifferent or even hostile land.[7] For all my skepticism about their image as *the* picture of the church for our time, as *a* picture it is very compelling. In a time when we cannot take Christendom for granted, there is good news in the portrait of a community that knows who it is and what it does, a community marked by particular and sometimes even peculiar practices. In a time that we call postmodern (God knows what our grandchildren will call it), and in which it seems that the options for living and believing are unlimited, we still do, all of us, have to make our way through life as surely as the children of Israel had to make their way to Canaan and as Matthew's church had to make their way to the kingdom. It is good news to know that there are certain guideposts on the way.

Paul Minear captures beautifully the sense in which the Matthean way also provides a world:

> [In Matthew] a new map of both the heavens and the earth becomes accessible to God's family on earth. So when we listen intently to the Gospel, when we accept the good news of God's kingdom, when we join in the petitions of the Lord's Prayer, when we receive the Passover body and blood, the gift of grace becomes as amazing as the apostles declared it to be. The shock of receiving that grace is greater than any culture shock, ancient or modern.[8]

### Kingdom in the Indicative

While it is clear that Matthew's Gospel is dominated by the imperative, we note that even in the Sermon on the Mount, when Jesus begins to speak of the kingdom he speaks in the indicative, and at the heart of that Sermon he invites disciples to prayerful trust. Jesus' ministry of proclamation begins with the Sermon on the Mount, and the Sermon on the Mount begins with the Beatitudes, which set the focus for the Sermon. Of course, and above all, the Beatitudes are words of assurance and promise for the disciples and for the crowds who may become disciples. But the words are assuring and promising only because they point to the power of God to make good on promises.

If God were not God, the Beatitudes would be only piety and platitude. They are *not* piety and platitude only because God has the power to perform the blessings that Jesus proclaims. The poor in spirit will inherit the kingdom because the King wishes to make them God's heirs. Those who mourn will be comforted because God is comforter. Those who are lowly will be lifted up because God has the power to raise them up; and those who hunger and thirst after righteousness will be filled only because they seek after the God who is right and just.

Some of the worst sermons I have heard have tried to turn the Beatitudes into a set of rules: Humble your spirit; seek righteousness. The imperative is implicit here, of course, but the blessing is explicit, and the grounding of that blessing is this good news: God can perform what God promises, and what God promises is astonishingly bright and fair. As I began by acknowledging Calvin as a wise reader of these texts, let me cite Luther on this text: "Blessed are the poor in spirit, for theirs is the kingdom of heaven." Luther says, "This is a fine, sweet and friendly beginning for Christ's instruction and preaching. He does not come like Moses or a teacher of the Law, with demands, threats and terrors, but in a very friendly way, with enticements, allurements, and pleasant promises."[9]

If we see the Beatitudes as God's great indicative claim about God's own blessedness and the blessedness of those whom God chooses to bless, then, just as with Paul's letters, the Sermon on the Mount lets imperative follow from indicative: As blessed children of the blessed God, here is how you are to live. So we need to demur a bit from Ulrich Luz's claim that in Matthew the imperative always precedes and dominates; it does dominate, but at least in the Sermon on the Mount it does not precede. It follows the great indicatives: Blessed are they . . . blessed are you.

Notice something else about the Sermon on the Mount, this paradigm of Gospel for Matthew, and again I owe this insight to Ulrich Luz. However you figure the center of the Sermon (whether you simply count the verses or engage in an elaborate study of the chiastic structure of the Sermon), what you find at the middle of the Sermon on the Mount is prayer, the Lord's Prayer.[10] So, at the center of a discourse that seems to begin with blessing but end with demand there is an absolute commitment to trust. To be sure, God turns to us in the preaching of Jesus, but to be sure we also turn to God, trusting that God hears, guides, and forgives. The sovereign king of heaven is also "Our Father." Whether "Abba" is Jesus' unique term, and whether it means "Daddy" or "Distinguished Progenitor," doesn't matter nearly so much as the fact that at the center of all this sovereignty and power there is the personal care of God.

Heaven impinges on earth. "Your kingdom come. Your will be done, on earth as it is in heaven" (Matt. 6:10). The coming of the kingdom and the doing of the will are inseparable. God reigns and we are servants of that reign. The line between transcendence and immanence, between the sublime and the mundane, disappears. "Give us this day our daily bread" (Matt. 6:11). I know nobody can make the exegesis work, but this bread has got to be manna. Here is the new Moses on the new mountain, telling us that if we trust God for each day, we'll have enough for each day and when we ask for more we tilt toward pride.

Frederick Buechner tells of that day when he was about to give up on the sovereignty of God and his own self-confidence because his beloved daughter was suffering anorexia, and no effort, prayer, or therapy seemed to avail. So he pulled off the road just to gather his strength and noticed the car going by on the highway with one of those vanity plates, which in this case was not vanity but gospel: "Trust," it said, just Trust.[11]

Right in the middle of the Sermon on the Mount, with its stress on the God who reigns and our obligation to serve, is that prayer which is the absolute and inescapable sign, the license by which we live our lives as Christian people: Trust.

## The Gospel of Expensive Grace

So for Matthew, gospel is the gospel of the kingdom, and indeed, at the beginning of Jesus' ministry Matthew takes the word of the kingdom as a substitute for Mark's use of the term "gospel." When Jesus begins to preach, the good news is the good news of the blessings that the kingdom does and will bestow—beatitudes. There is imperative, and there is indicative, and both contain or imply good news.

The end of Matthew's Gospel also does something slightly different from what we might expect. In the first great commission of Matthew's Gospel, when Jesus sends the disciples out among the people of Israel he says, "As you go, proclaim the good news, 'The kingdom of heaven has come near'" (Matt. 10:7). (Note how explicitly good news and kingdom come together.) In the second great commission, when Jesus sends the disciples out among the nations, he says, "Go . . . make disciples . . . , baptizing them . . . , and teaching them to obey." Good news has become discipleship and teaching.

Now for Matthew, parallel to preaching the gospel, one might even say central to preaching the gospel, is making disciples. C. H. Dodd's distinction between kerygma and *didache* will not hold for the end of Matthew's Gospel or for the Gospel itself: preaching is teaching and the good news is the call to obedience.[12] It is not that one declares what God has done in Christ and then gives instructions for how to live in Christian community. What God has done in Christ is to call people to obedience and into community. Teaching about Christ's kingdom is the good news of Christ's kingdom.

Take two of the little parables that end Matthew 13—parables that Matthew has added to his Markan source (Matt. 13:44–46). Remember that for Matthew the good news is the good news of the kingdom. In one of these parables the kingdom is like a treasure hidden in a field: the one who finds the treasure is called to discipleship—to sell all that he has for the sake of the treasure. In another parable the kingdom is like a pearl of great price, and the one who finds the pearl shows his obedience in two ways: by the zeal with which he searches for the jewel and by the audacity with which he reorients his life to buy the treasure he has found. When Jesus tells his disciples to make disciples, he urges them to enlist and teach people who will know how to recognize the kingdom when they stumble on it; he urges them to enlist and teach people who will have the courage to seek what is immeasurably good, who will have the courage to be disciples.

Dietrich Bonhoeffer, who in the last century stood as the great sign against an easy rush toward an easy gospel, remained from first to last an advocate of the centrality of grace. When he insisted that God's grace was not cheap grace but expensive grace, he reminded us that it was still grace that was expensive: not some strategy by which we attained what was still inescapably a gift, a surprise. We remember what Bonhoeffer said about cheap grace:

> Cheap grace is the preaching of forgiveness without requiring repentance, baptism without church discipline, Communion without confession. . . . Cheap grace is grace without discipleship, grace without the cross, grace without Jesus Christ, living and incarnate.

But we forget what he said about the grace that is costly, but grace all the same:

> Costly grace is the treasure hidden in the field; for the sake of it a man will gladly go and sell all that he has. It is the pearl of great price to buy for which the merchant will sell all his goods. It is the kingly rule of Christ, for whose sake a man will pluck out the eye which causes him to stumble, it is the call of Jesus Christ at which the disciple leaves his nets and follows him.[13]

One might draw the analogy of a marriage or a great romance: If you fall in love and the beloved loves you without hesitation in return, that is a great gift. If you fall in love and have to move heaven and earth to win the devotion of the beloved—that devotion is still a great gift. Treasure you stumble on in the field is a treasure; treasure sought far and wide, finally found in the shop and purchased at great price, is still a treasure. Paul would have a harder time with the second kind of gift, but for Matthew and Bonhoeffer both are gifts. (See Matt. 13:44–46.)

## The Kingdom and the End

If the gospel in Matthew is always the gospel of the kingdom, then we need also to note that the gospel carries with it an eschatological note. The first great sermon of Matthew's Gospel begins with a series of promises: "Blessed are those who mourn, for they will be comforted." "Blessed are the peacemakers, for they will be called children of God." "Blessed are the pure in heart, for they will see God." These are not promises about the way the world goes. Comfort will not come through grief therapy; the peacemakers will probably be called troublemakers in tomorrow's paper; the pure in heart will do well to see hints of God, through a glass darkly.

The last great sermon in this Gospel, in Matthew 24–25, ends with a series of stories about what the final consummation will look like: like a bridegroom coming to the wedding feast, like a landowner coming back to check on his investments, like a shepherd separating sheep from goats.

In these sermons, Matthew and Paul come together. The good news is good news not only of what God has done; the good news is the promise of God's consummation. Nonetheless, in the mainline or old-line churches we find eschatology hard to deal with. In the lectures on systematic theology I heard when I was a student at this divinity school years ago, Julian Hartt unfortunately ran out of time before he could get to those lectures on eschatology that he had planned. And Karl Barth never finished the final volumes of his *Dogmatics*, the volumes that were supposed to deal with last things. Whatever was going on with those two theologians psychologically, parabolically they demonstrated what they did not lecture or write on: time is always running out.

For three thousand and more of our fellow humans, time suddenly ran out on September 11, 2001. Matthew's Gospel knows that, that time is always running out. What we do in time will be consummated beyond time. Our timely faithfulness will be blessed and our timely shortcomings will be judged.

I am no better at preaching eschatology at sixty than I was when I was twenty-six, but I feel its pull more strongly. I do not think our preaching describes the furniture of heaven or the temperature of hell, but I do know that there is unfulfilled longing and unmitigated suffering in the world in which we live and among the people to whom we preach. Matthew's promise of the future, of a kingdom that is on its way but yet to come, provides continuing good news.

Furthermore, especially for those people whose lives are marked more by oppression than by blessing, people much like Matthew's original audience, the promise that God's future will provide comfort and release is almost a necessary correlation of the promise that God is really God. Otherwise any score sheet of the day's victories and losses can leave the oppressed still with the strong sense that some other power is in control.

Of course, Matthew's eschatological pull has strong implications for how we live in this world. The prayer's great petition, "Your will be done, on earth as it is in heaven," is partly the promise to serve faithfully in the present what will be completed only in the future. The three great stories of Matthew 25 tell us to be faithful as we await the bridegroom, courageous with the talent we have been given, compassionate to those who suffer hunger, imprisonment, and loss and who are Christ's brothers and sisters. But in each case we are obedient both to a demand and to a promise. The wedding will be celebrated, the landowner will return, the shepherd will bless the good and faithful servants. The beatitudes are both eschatological promises and daily reminders. The command to pray for the enemy is a word that is always hardest and most necessary in apocalyptic times.

Nicholas Wolterstorff in his remarkable book *Lament for a Son*, written after the death of Clare's and his son, Eric, talks about how the beatitude lays hold of the future but shapes the present too:

> "Blessed are those who mourn?" What can it mean? One can understand why Jesus hails those who hunger and thirst for righteousness, why he hails the merciful, why he hails the pure in heart, why he hails the peacemakers, why he hails those who endure under persecution. These are qualities of character which belong to the life of the kingdom. But why does he hail the mourners of the world? Why cheer tears? It must be that mourning is also a quality of character that belongs to the life of his realm.
>
> Who then are the mourners? The mourners are those who have caught a glimpse of God's new day, who ache with all their being for that day's coming, and who break out into tears when confronted with its absence. They are the ones who realize that in God's realm of peace there is no one blind and who ache whenever they see someone unseeing . . . They are the ones who realize that in God's realm there is no one without dignity and who ache whenever they see someone treated with indignity. They are the ones who realize that in God's realm of peace there is neither death nor tears and who ache whenever they see someone crying tears over death. The mourners are aching visionaries.[14]

Preaching the good news in Matthew will require that we neither attend entirely to God's demands for this present age nor preach hope unrelated to responsibility. What we as preachers bind on earth is also bound in heaven: Jesus tells Peter that when he asserts that Peter is the Rock. God's present will and God's coming kingdom are inextricably bound together. (See Matt. 16:18–19.)

## Gospel: God with Us

Finally, there is good news in Matthew because Matthew's Gospel begins and ends with a promise. Here is the promise at the beginning: "They shall name him Emmanuel, which means 'God is with us'" (Matt. 1:23). Here is the promise at the end: "Remember, I am with you always, to the end of the age" (Matt. 28:20).

While it is clear that the fullness of the good news awaits the consummation of God's promises, it is also clear that in the meantime we are sustained by the presence of the Christ who is with us.

Of course he is present partly as teacher and guide. The Christ who made disciples and guided them in the way of righteousness makes disciples still and guides as well. The much-quoted promise of Matthew 18:20, "For where two or three are gathered in my name, I am there among them," is not a promise that Christ will be there to make us feel good in tough times. It is a promise that Christ is present to us in making the hard decisions that come with church discipline, with complicated obedience.

But he is present as sustainer and encourager as well. Matthew's telling of the two miracles of Jesus on the sea suggest this, as Günther Bornkamm noted years ago.[15] Whether Matthew foresaw the early church's interpretation that the ship on the stormy sea in Matthew 8:23–27 foreshadowed the church in its times of trouble, he did foresee that faith is often mixed with fear and that faithful people need to turn to Immanuel, crying, "Lord, help!" and help will come. Similarly, while in the story of Christ walking on the water in Matthew 14:22–33 it is true that Peter is chided for his "little faith," it is also true that that "little faith" becomes faith enough when Christ reaches out to bring the wavering disciple safely to the boat and calms the storm.

There is another sign of "God with us" in Matthew's Gospel, as well. In the first great section of the Gospel, and especially in the Sermon on the Mount, Jesus reveals to the disciples the new law, or the new interpretation of the law, that is fulfilled in him. But, he says, "Do not think that I have come to abolish the law or the prophets; I have come not to abolish but to fulfill" (Matt. 5:17). In Matthew 11, just before moving to the section on the parables and the kingdom, Jesus makes clear that he embodies the law that he enjoins. This is Matthew's version of John's prologue:

for John the Word is made flesh; for Matthew Torah is made flesh. And what is perhaps implicit in the great sermon becomes explicit in the great assurance. Torah is not primarily daily burden but—astonishingly—Sabbath rest:

> Come to me, all you that are weary and are carrying heavy burdens, and I will give you rest. Take my yoke upon you, and learn from me; for I am gentle and humble in heart, and you will find rest for your souls. (Matt. 11:28–29)

Matthew's Gospel is chock-full of gospel as demand, but every once in a while we are reminded of the promise too. That the one who demands is present to help in our obedience. That sometimes little faith is accepted and transformed as if it were full faith.

Years ago when our sons were small, our family was on a camping trip. Before dinner I went with the boys to the camp restroom to wash up for the meal. After we had washed our hands, I reached up to the towel dispenser to get a paper towel for each of the boys, but our younger son protested loudly: "I can do it myself."

Since he was rather short and the towel dispenser rather high, I puzzled what would happen next until he made it clear: "Come on, Daddy, lift me up so I can do it myself."

In Matthew's Gospel, Jesus Christ, Immanuel, calls us to costly grace and difficult discipleship. But he also lifts us to obey.

Good news.

*Sermon*

# The Wise and the Foolish

## MATTHEW 25:1–13

We cannot watch television or listen to the radio or read the newspapers without knowing that a new millennium is coming. Whether or not the early historian was right who guessed that Jesus got born right as 1 B.C. turned into 1 A.D., there is something exciting about having a year called "2000." It sounds like the start of something big.

We also all rely on computers, whether we have our own computer or not. The banks use computers and the post office and grocery stores and all kinds of transportation. There is considerable worry that some people and some businesses won't really be ready when the millennium comes, because their computers won't be upgraded to be ready for the new century. The computers will just crash.

The point is that we'd better be ready when things change. That is the point of the story Jesus tells in Matthew's Gospel, too.

When Matthew wrote his Gospel, people weren't waiting for the new millennium, they were waiting for Christ to come again. They did not know when that would happen, and perhaps some did not think seriously about what it might mean for Jesus to come again, so Matthew reminds them of this story of Jesus about another group of people who were waiting.

Just as Matthew's first readers were supposed to be waiting for Jesus, the ten bridesmaids in his story were waiting for the bridegroom to come. They had been invited to the wedding, but for whatever reason the bridegroom did not get there right at the time listed on the invitation.

The wise bridesmaids knew that that is often how it goes with grooms—not always absolutely reliable when it comes to their

Preached at Central Baptist Church, Hartford, Connecticut, on November 9, 1999.

timetable. So just in case the wedding didn't take place right on schedule, they brought extra oil to get them through the night. The foolish bridesmaids were just as excited about the wedding as the wise ones, but they were not as prudent or foresighted. They brought just enough oil to get them up to the official time of the wedding, and when the wedding was delayed, they were in trouble.

Now it is true that some Christians in 1999 are just as sure Jesus will come again soon as some Christians were in about 79, when Matthew wrote his Gospel. Some think that we don't need to worry about whether our computers make it into the next millennium, because Jesus will come in glory and banks and post offices and grocery stores and airports won't matter any more.

My own guess is that history will go on right past the beginning of the millennium, and while I think that the end of history is in God's hands, I also do not think that that end will come any time very soon.

But I do think that just as the bridegroom shows up when the bridesmaids have stopped paying attention, Christ shows up in our lives. Not in clouds of glory, but in the life of the church, in the needs of a neighbor, in our own struggle for faith. There is Jesus saying: "Are you ready? Are you wise or are you foolish? Have you got enough oil?"

What seems odd about this story in Matthew's Gospel is that the wise bridesmaids seem more than a little selfish. So often in the Gospel does Jesus remind us to share that it seems odd that at this point, at this crisis, he points out that the wise bridesmaids won't share one drop of their oil.

But of course the story isn't just about oil and bridesmaids. It's about how prepared we are for those moments when we face Jesus' demands and Jesus' promises. When Christ comes near.

You remember the old spiritual, "Not my sister nor my brother, but it's me, O Lord, standing in the need of prayer. Not the preacher or the deacon, but it's me, O Lord, standing in the need of prayer."

Here's a tough fact about the Christian faith. There are lots of things we can do for each other. There's a lot you can do for me. But you can't get ready for Jesus for me. You can't use your faith instead of my faith—and while I want you to pray for me, you can't pray instead of me. In each of our lives there are ways that we and only we can get ourselves ready. By praying steadfastly, by growing in hope, by coming to church, by reading the Bible expectantly. Keeping the oil ready for our lamps.

This cannot be an easy time in the life of this church. It's always difficult when a pastor leaves, because we rely on our pastors to strengthen us in faith and hope. They help us keep the oil ready.

But they can't do it for us. Not even the best minister can do it for us. They can share their faith and keep us in their prayers, but their faith doesn't replace our faith and their prayers are no substitute for our own.

This is a time of waiting and a time of preparation, and it may be a time of blessedness too. I've been a pastor, and I noticed that in the interims before I arrived and after I left, what was pretty clear all along got really clear.

A time of loss is also a time of strength. People are better prepared than they think to lead and to serve. There is oil enough for the lamps God has given us. When the next senior pastor comes, you will be ready to work with her or him as fellow servants and fellow leaders, too.

So that's it, the heart of what our passage from Matthew tells us. Keep faith; keep hope; keep praying and worshiping. Nobody else can do it for you. When the time of crisis or surprise or amazement comes, be ready.

But there are two P.S.s, two additions that Matthew makes in his Gospel that help us understand this story better. One is the P.S. at the very end of this chapter. Jesus tells another story, this one about people who are in need of food and drink and companionship and care. Listen, he says, whenever you take care of one of the least of these, my brothers and sisters, you take care of me.

That is a reminder that while there are some things Christians can do only for themselves, there are equally important things that we can do for others. You cannot give someone else your faith, or study the Bible in their place, or be their proxy at worship. But to the hungry you can give food, to the lonely your companionship, to the homeless shelter.

To be sure, we need to be like the wise bridesmaids and attend to the faith that is ours; but we also need to be like Christ himself, who did not simply hang on to what was his, but gave love and compassion and kindness and finally his very self.

Which brings me to the second P.S. After all this speech is over, the story about the bridesmaids and the story about helping the least of these as well, after that Jesus invites the disciples and invites us to a feast. It's a feast of sorrow but also a feast of joy; a feast of loss but also a feast of celebration.

Truth is, he does what he says we cannot easily do for each other. He gives us oil for our lamps and bread for our journey and the cup for the thirst of our souls.

His broken body and his spilled blood sustain us through the long days and the weary nights. "This is my body," he says. "This is my blood."

And through his mercy he turns the days of our lives into his marriage feast of love.

Amen.

*Chapter Four*

# The Gospel in Luke:
# Forgiveness and Justice

Historically, Matthew has been the church's Gospel, and I think for the last thirty years or so Mark and John have been the scholars' Gospels. But Luke is the people's Gospel.

How could it not be so when people who don't get to church very often do manage to get there for the Christmas pageant? Even if they have forgotten everything else, they still remember that the sign of peace among those with whom God is well pleased is a baby, wrapped in swaddling clothes, and lying in a manger. And how could it not be so with the two stories everyone knows, the good Samaritan and the prodigal son? Both parables are perhaps mistitled, but both are so engraved on the popular imagination that innumerable hospitals are called "Good Samaritan," and a chain of campgrounds is named "Good Sam." Everyone has a vague idea of what it might be to wander as a prodigal or to return to a fatted calf. In a book with contemporary poems reflecting on Gospel passages that I was given, there was at most a poem or two for any number of passages—and seven retelling the story of the prodigal son.

Of course, when people have the birth narrative and the two parables, they actually have a good piece of what makes the Gospel good news for the author of Luke and Acts.

## The Good News of the Messiah's Birth

Luke's Gospel, unlike Matthew's, never uses the noun "gospel" at all. We return to this phenomenon toward the end of the chapter to see if there are reasons deeper than vocabulary choice that lie behind it. But what Luke does use again and again is the verb "to preach the gospel." (Matthew uses the verb only once. Mark uses the noun eight times but never uses the verb.) Whereas in Matthew it is Jesus who first preaches the good news, in Luke the good news is first preached *about* Jesus.

The variety of translations of the term "to preach good news" (*euaggelizesthai*) hide the clarity of the claim. For Luke, the gospel, the good news, is first of all the story of the Christ's advent. Knowing the nativity story is a good way of beginning to know what counts for Luke as good news. When Gabriel appears to Zechariah, he "gospels" him, preaches the gospel: "I have been sent," says the angel, using the verb that lies behind the term "apostle." "I [have been apostled] am God's apostle," says the angel, "and I have come to bring you good news" (Luke 1:19). The good news is most immediately the news that Elizabeth and Zechariah will have a son, but as the son foreshadows his cousin, this good news foreshadows the greater good news that in the birth of John the Baptist the coming of God's Messiah is begun (Luke 1: 19).

When the angels appear to the shepherds and tell them not to fear, the angels go on to preach the gospel: "I preach to you good news of great joy" (Luke 2:10). The good news is the birth of the Savior; the sign of the good news is the baby wrapped in swaddling clothes and lying in the manger. (Remember that in Galatians 1:6–8 Paul was perfectly glad to have angels preach the gospel, just so they didn't try to preach some gospel different from his own.) And when John the Baptist begins his preaching, though it is full of judgment and admonition, because it prepares the way of the greater one who follows, Luke tells us that John "preaches the good news" (Luke 3:18).

Rudolf Bultmann has said that in the development of Christian tradition, Jesus the proclaimer becomes the proclaimed.[1] It is perhaps too simple but nonetheless a useful distinction between Matthew's understanding of the gospel of the kingdom and Luke's understanding of the good news about Jesus to say that the proclaimer has become the proclaimed.

All this is to say what we said at the beginning, that those who remember Luke because they remember the birth narrative have at least this right: the good news is good news because it is news about the child born in the manger, who of course becomes the complicated and compelling master and Lord.

## Good News to the Poor

As with Matthew, when Jesus preaches the gospel in Luke's Gospel, Jesus also preaches "the kingdom." In Luke 4:43, Jesus tells the disciples that his job is to preach the good news of the kingdom in all the towns around. But Luke also specifies, as Matthew does not, that good news of the kingdom is good news to the poor. Jesus' inaugural speech in the synagogue at Nazareth spells out what Luke thinks is contained in Jesus' own preaching of the gospel.[2] The passage from Isaiah becomes the program for Jesus' ministry:

> The Spirit of the Lord is upon me,
> because he has anointed me to bring good news to the poor . . .
> [and] to proclaim release to the captives.
>
> (Luke 4:18)

As everyone notes, when Luke comes to his version of Jesus' great speech on discipleship—the Sermon on the Plain for Matthew's Sermon on the Mount—he also shows us that Jesus begins with blessings, promises of the sovereignty of God. But the blessings are a little different: not "Blessed are the poor in spirit" but "Blessed are you . . . poor" (Matt. 5:3; Luke 6:20). And the other side of blessing is explicit in the woes pronounced on those who are wealthy or at the very least on those who trust in their wealth: "Woe to you who are rich, for you have received your consolation" (Luke 6:24).

If, as I suggested in the chapter on Matthew, the Beatitudes tell us not just something about those who are blessed but something about the God who blesses, in Luke we have a God who blesses in part through overturning the structures of society and making a brand-new world. Mary, who is in many ways the first human evangelist in Luke's Gospel, the first preacher of the gospel (after the angelic preacher addresses Zechariah and Mary herself), declares what is a promise directed especially to the downcast and the outcast.

> He has shown strength with his arm,
>> he has scattered the proud in the thoughts of their hearts.
> He has brought down the powerful from their thrones,
>> and lifted up the lowly;
> he has filled the hungry with good things,
>> and sent the rich away empty.
>
> (Luke 1:51–53)

Some years ago when I was teaching in Virginia I taught a class on preaching social issues; I taught the class both for Union/Presbyterian School of Christian Education, a primarily Euramerican seminary, and for Virginia Union, a predominantly African American seminary. By happy coincidence or providence, our class had Africans from Ghana, African Americans, a Hispanic Ph.D. student from Puerto Rico, a Korean student, and a mix of fairly Anglo Americans. One book we chose to read was Robert McAfee Brown's *Unexpected News.*[3] The Bible spoke to us again because we were asked to see the Bible through eyes not our own, especially the eyes of people in the developing world. We preached sermons based on the Bible, but influenced by our conversations with one another and our reading of Brown. A woman named Mary, who had come to us from Ghana, preached the sermon I still remember best.

Her text was the Magnificat: "When I read about this other Mary," said our Mary, "I think about myself. I am a poor person in a poor country. A woman in a culture that does not greatly value women. A Christian where the churches have not looked often to women for leadership. And my church said to me, go to the United States, study to become a minister, come home and lead us." Then, said Mary, in the words of that earlier Mary: "Oh, my soul doth magnify the Lord."

A Lukan text produced a Lukan sermon. Perhaps more than any other Gospel writer, Luke knew that his good news was unexpected news.

The parable of the good Samaritan is not just about niceness, it is about justice and the God who works to make things right. Those who remember the parable *do* remember a good piece of Luke's Gospel. In the framework for the parable Jesus turns the question around: "Who is my neighbor?" the lawyer asks, putting Jesus to the test. "Be a neighbor," says Jesus, putting the test to the lawyer himself. In the parable Jesus turns the world around. The Samaritan, the one despised and rejected, turns out to be the one who acts neighborly. Alan Culpepper gets it right, I think: "By depicting a Samaritan as the hero of the story . . . Jesus demolished all boundary expectations. Social position—race, religion, or region—count for nothing. "[4]

The good news is that those who seem to be outside are brought inside; they are key players in God's story.

The good news is that the neighborhood that might have seemed to be limited to those who share the same religion or the same race or the same history is as large as the providence of God.

The good news (which as with Matthew is also hard news) is that we are called to be neighbors, not just to the obvious candidates, but to the needy who don't seem like our neighbors at all. Need we say that in this time when we have seen our immediate neighborhood violated and our national neighborhood threatened, the Christian call reminds us that the neighborhood is bigger than America the beautiful, much as we may love this land—that to be a believer in Allah is just to be an Arabic-speaking believer in God. We who have been the victims of terrible, rude violence are sometimes implicated in terrible polite violence, or at the very least avert our eyes and march by very quickly on the other side. The parable reminds us of that.

The debate among critics goes on concerning the social location of Luke's Gospel and the program he has in mind. Does he write out of a preferential option for the poor, or does he write for the wealthy, reminding them of their obligation to live charitably? What seems to be beyond dispute is that the vision of a history reshaped by the power of God is Luke's contribution to the understanding of gospel. Preaching that looks to God's vindication of God's people as an eschatological promise that also shapes the movement of history itself rightly looks to Luke-Acts. Acts says it's the world turned upside down (Acts 17:6), and in Luke-Acts we are certainly on the way to that turning. Mary, the unmarried woman, bears a Savior. Paul, the persecutor of the church, becomes Christ's missionary; Cornelius the Gentile joins the family of Abraham; the gospel spreads from small Jerusalem to great Rome.

Then as we move from Luke to Acts it also becomes clear that there is a more particular locus for the world turned upside down. Church becomes a parable, a firstfruits of the world turned upside down. The initial optimistic picture of the church as a community where all things are held in common may fade by the end of the story. But what is clear is that the church remains a community where the walls between rich and poor, between Jew and Gentile, are broken down.

The familiar line is that the eschatological expectation that so shapes the gospel in Paul and Matthew has somewhat diminished by the time Luke writes his two volumes. Luke can write a history of the church because he assumes that church will go on and that its history will count. It is not, however, that the kingdom disappears and that the church takes its place, as some accounts of the tradition would have it; it is rather that while the kingdom's fullness is yet to be accomplished, the church becomes an ongoing testimony to the kingdom's coming power and its present blessing. Take, for example, the best-known sermon in Acts, Peter's sermon at Pentecost:

> This is what was spoken through the prophet Joel:
> "In the last days it will be, God declares,
>     that I will pour out my Spirit upon all flesh."
>
> (Acts 2:16–17)

Of course Peter's sermon describes the Pentecost experience as the outpouring of the Holy Spirit. But more than that—in quoting Joel, Peter assures the listeners that this gift of the Spirit is a sign of the last days. Maybe we are right in understanding Pentecost as the birthday of the church, but we do well to remember that the church born on that day is an eschatological community: it is the interim holding company until the kingdom turns the world upside down.

## The Gospel of Forgiveness

In one of his earliest novels, *The Final Beast*, Frederick Buechner, who is, I think, the only Beecher lecturer who is also a fine novelist, tells the story of a young minister named Roy Nicolet, who is trying to figure out how to be a minister. Figuring out how to be a minister includes figuring out what to say when he preaches. The most puzzling member of his flock is a young woman named Rooney. He knows that Rooney has been involved in a brief and loveless extramarital affair, and he notices that she wanders into church sporadically for reasons she cannot herself explain. Nicolet at least knows enough to know his own ignorance, and wisely turns to Lillian Flagg, a layperson who knows more about Rooney and more about faith than the preacher does.

"What can I tell Rooney?" asks Roy.

Here is what Lillian Flagg says: "She doesn't know God forgives her. That's the only power you have—to tell her that. Not just that he forgives her poor little adultery. But the faces she can't bear to look at now. . . . Tell her he forgives her for being lonely and bored, for not being full of joy with a houseful of children. . . . Tell her that sin is forgiven because whether she knows it or not, that's what she wants more than anything else—what all of us want. What on earth do you think you were ordained for?"[5]

The strong stress on the gospel as the forgiveness of sins is particularly evident in Luke's Gospel and to some extent in the book of Acts. I suggested in chapter 3, on Matthew, that one way to see what Matthew thinks is central to proclamation is to look at the end of his Gospel, the so-called Great Commission that Jesus provides the disciples. When Matthew's disciples go out to Israel they are to preach the good news of the kingdom. When they take their message to the world they are to make disciples and to teach all nations to obey.

Luke, too, ends with a kind of great commission, and again we can look at Jesus' words in that commission for a clue to what he understands good news to be for his time and for his people. In Luke 24:45–49, Jesus, as preacher, is interpreting the Scripture to the disciples:

> Then he helped them understand the Scriptures. He told them:
>
> "The Scriptures say that the Messiah must suffer, then three days later he will rise from death. They also say that repentance and forgiveness of sins must be preached to all nations. You are my witnesses, beginning in Jerusalem. I will send you the Spirit the Father has promised, but you must remain in the city until you are given power from heaven."
> (Author's paraphrase)

The theme of forgiveness permeates the narratives of Luke and Acts. Only in Luke's Gospel does the crucified Christ ask forgiveness for those who have crucified him. In Acts, Stephen asks forgiveness for those who are executing him. In Acts, too, almost all the apostolic sermons end with the injunction to repent and receive forgiveness. In retelling his conversion, or call, in the book of Acts, Paul says that he was instructed by Ananias to "be baptized, and have your sins washed away" (Acts 22:16).

I said earlier that those who know the birth narrative, the good Samaritan story, and the prodigal son story know more of Luke's good news than they may realize. The most famous of all parables, found in Luke alone, is the story of the prodigal son, which of course is also the story of the elder brother, which of course is also the story of the forgiving father. In its context in Jesus' ministry the parable certainly had to do, in part, with the ability or inability of those who thought they were saved to welcome sinners; in its context in Luke's Gospel it has to do in part with opening up a church for Gentiles and Jews alike.

However, as preachers have also known for centuries, the parable is the paradigmatic picture of a God who is so willing to forgive that God looks like a father, putting aside all divine dignity and running down the road to greet the son who has wandered into the far country. It is the paradigmatic picture of a God so willing to forgive, that like a father, he puts aside all divine reticence and heads to the fields where the elder brother has turned the family farm into his own far country, to beg him to come to the party, to come home. Jesus friend of sinners is Luke's Jesus. What Lillian Flagg wants Buechner's Roy Nicolet to preach is a Lukan sermon.

After all these years I would testify that it does not matter as much as I once thought it did whether one begins with Gospel and in the light of Gospel preaches judgment and then moves to reconciliation, as Karl Barth would enjoin, or whether one starts with judgment and moves to Gospel, as Jonathan Edwards and generations of revivalist preachers since have done. The people in our pews may not know the name for judgment, but they know its reality. The passage I remembered most vividly from Gene Bartlett's 1961 Beecher Lectures was vivid still in the rereading: "Judgment is to live by the sensual until we become increasingly satiated and decreasingly satisfied. . . . Judgment is to live an ever-contracting life, drawing in and trusting no one until at last we trust least of all ourselves. . . . It is to see through everything until we see into nothing. It is the distorted vision, the bound affection, the broken relationship, the servitude to appetite, the point at which we live as we do, not because we may but because we must."[6] This frantic scurry is not real life; nor is the bored indifference that is its other side. Our people often do not know that God forgives them for being bored with a job that enervates and a family that puzzles and a church that seems marginal to their needs. They do not know God forgives them, and we can tell them that, or what on earth do we think we were ordained for?

## Witnesses to the Gospel

The Great Commission at the end of Matthew calls for the disciples to make disciples and to teach obedience. The great commission at the end of Luke calls for the apostles to preach forgiveness and to serve as witnesses.

For Luke, preaching the gospel is a matter of bearing witness. At the beginning of Acts, after the death of Judas, the apostles need to find a twelfth person to bear witness (Acts 1:15–26). Bearing witness requires two things. First, one must testify to the resurrection. Second, one must have been with Jesus from the beginning of his ministry, must have been a witness in the legal sense, so that asked to testify one may say: I was there; here's how it happened. One must be an eyewitness.

(This is why Paul is almost never an apostle in Acts; his testimony was true, but he was not an eyewitness to the ministry, beginning in Galilee. Paul presumably would have said that Galilean memories were mostly about Jesus according to the flesh anyway, and that he'd seen all anybody needed to see to be an apostle: the risen Lord. Not only would he presumably have said that, he pretty much did say it in 1 Corinthians 9 and 2 Corinthians 5.)

Of course, by the time Luke wrote Acts the original circle of apostles had nearly all died, and Luke knew perfectly well that the witness of the church could no longer depend on the testimony of eyewitnesses. The question is, what would it mean for the apostolic testimony, witness, to continue after the apostles were gone? Not surprisingly, I have a fairly low-church answer to that question.

Christian witness continues to require two things. First, Christian witness must be true, that is, it must be congruent with the preaching of the apostles, and especially it must be true to the claim that God has vindicated Jesus as Messiah by raising him from the dead. Second, Christian witness must be based on what the preacher has actually witnessed in her own life—not only on the reports she has received from others. Though Luke does not explicitly use the word "witness" in explaining how the testimony continues past the death of the apostles, implicitly he does ground

Christian testimony in the lives of those who testify as well as in the tradition of the church.

In the great story of the Emmaus meal, it is clear how the risen Lord is made known to the two disciples and by extension to the church that continues long after they are gone. He is made known in the interpretation of Scripture and in the breaking of bread.

Sharon Ringe points out the way in which past and present come together in the words of Jesus to the disciples:

> Both Jesus' words and the interpretation of scripture join the symbolic meal to give liturgical shape to the events. The verb tenses—"These *are* my words that I *spoke*"—establish continuity between what Jesus said and what the risen Christ says [Luke 24:44a; italics Ringe's]. . . .The reference to the law of Moses, the prophets, the psalms, and Jesus' words about his own fate and about the church's mission (24:44b-47) establish the continuity of God's saving purpose that encompasses both Israel and the Gentiles. That continuity is to be the subject of their witness (21:12–15), for which they will be empowered just as Jesus was empowered for his own ministry.[7]

It is not as though when the church comes together to hear the word proclaimed and to share the meal we become secondhand interpreters of a story that rightly belongs to generations long gone. It is rather that we become witnesses to that reality to which we bear witness. The life of the preacher, like the life of every Christian, is nurtured in word and sacrament. We receive in order that we may share. (See Luke 24:13–35.)

In the narrative that in many ways is the conclusion of the testimony about witnessing in Luke and Acts, Paul, who in some ways was himself already an heir of the apostles, passes on the ministry to his heirs, the Ephesian elders. In Acts 20 Paul admonishes the elders to serve as shepherds to the flock and to share the message with which they have been entrusted (see Acts 20:17–35). It is not only that the Ephesian elders have been witnesses to

Paul's ministry, it is also that they are themselves witnesses of the gospel. And of course throughout Luke and Acts, the promise of the Holy Spirit is precisely the promise that generations after the apostles will both know the story and know the reality of the gospel of forgiveness and justice that is preached to all nations.

In our basic preaching course at Yale we use Thomas Long's book *The Witness of Preaching*, and Long shows how preaching as witness helps us preach a gospel grounded in tradition, but also proven in our own life and ministry:

> The preacher as witness is not authoritative because of rank or power but rather because of what the preacher has seen and heard. When the preacher prepares a sermon by wrestling with a biblical text, the preacher is not merely gathering information about the text. The preacher is listening for a voice, looking for a presence, hoping for the claim of God to be encountered through the text.[8]

## The Gospel as Good News

In the first chapter I bore witness to the value of lectionary preaching in my own ministry. One of the gifts of having an assigned text is that it forces you to notice features of Scripture that you might never have noticed if you hadn't been forced to deal with that text. Now, in these lectures I assigned myself the question of what makes gospel gospel in various strains of Scripture, but having handed myself the assignment, I had to take it seriously, and in studying Luke–Acts I noticed something that otherwise I would have missed entirely: The noun "gospel," "*euaggelion,*" "good announcement," occurs not at all in Luke but only in Acts 15:7 and 20:24. That is, while there is plenty of preaching good tidings in Luke, there is nothing called "the gospel" until Acts. There is nothing called "the gospel" until Luke has finished writing *his* Gospel, or to put it differently, you don't have a Gospel until you can include in that Gospel the whole story Luke includes in Luke 1–24, from annunciation to resurrection.

In Acts 15:7, Peter says that he has been the apostle designated to preach the gospel, the good news, to the Gentiles. (We shall return to see what Peter's preaching looked like.) In Acts 20:24, Paul tells the Ephesian elders that his mission, about to come to an end, has also been to preach the good news.

One of the great gifts of literary criticism of Scripture is that when you haven't a clue to the original intention of the author, you can talk about the implied author, or the point that the text makes whether the author intended to or not. Put another way, I don't think Luke makes a big deal of the grammatical distinction between verb and noun, but the grammatical distinction points to a narrative strategy that is a very big deal indeed. The point I think this text makes, whether Luke knew it or not, is that for Luke *the* gospel is much like his Gospel. That is to say: the gospel is a story, and he shows that the gospel is a story.

Luke is famous for the stories he includes within his larger story. We have already remarked that the two parables everybody knows, the parable of the prodigal son and the parable of the good Samaritan, are stories Jesus tells in Luke's Gospel.

The greater attention to narrative preaching in our time grows in part out of greater attention to the way in which a story can itself carry the power of good news. We do not always have to stop and say, "Here is what this means for us today." The story told right can involve the hearer and proclaim the gospel of compassion.

Look at story, too, in the sermons of Acts. Peter in Acts 15 and Paul in Acts 20 tell their listeners that what they have been doing is preaching the gospel, the "noun," good news. When we see what they preach, we notice that it is a kind of narrative and that it follows something of the shape of the larger Gospel of Luke.

In Acts 3:12 Peter preaches a narrative summary of what good news looks like. It is a story set in the context of a larger story. The psalms and the prophecies of the Old Testament set the context for the newer narrative. The newer narrative is presented briefly. As we would have guessed from the way Luke's Gospel begins, the good news is first of all news about Jesus. The focus of the narrative is on the crucifixion and resurrection—in some ways the first twenty chapters of the Gospel of Luke are summed up in a single phrase: God has brought honor to his servant Jesus. The story of the crucifixion and resurrection are told both to indicate further the ways in which God has honored Jesus and to encourage what gospel preaching in Luke and Acts is so often to encourage: repentance and the acceptance of forgiveness of sins. As with the Gospel of Luke, the story looks beyond itself to the consummation of the narrative, when Jesus returns at a time yet to come. There is another way in which this narrative reflects the larger narrative of the Gospel: the man in Acts 3 who is healed by faith in Jesus recalls those miracles in the Gospel of Luke when faith is directly related to healing. Luke makes clear that in many ways the apostles prolong that story of God's mercy to those in distress: in the name of Jesus they did what Jesus did.

In Acts 13, where Paul explicitly preaches "good news" (13:32), the beginning and the end of the sermon place the story of Jesus in the context of the promises to Israel. Then Paul tells of the significance of John the Baptist and again moves quickly to the story of the arrest, trial, passion, and resurrection. As in the narrative of the Gospel itself, the point toward which the sermon drives is this: "My friends, the message is that Jesus can forgive your sins!" (13:38).

All this is to say that in Acts, when the apostles preach the gospel, the "gospel" they preach presents a kind of summary of the story of Luke's own Gospel. The promises of the first chapters of the Gospel—that the coming of Jesus fulfills Scripture, and that he is son of Abraham and son of David—is further spelled out by the citation of biblical promises. The story of arrest, trial, and crucifixion is narrated and explained: it provides the occasion for guilt and the opportunity for repentance and forgiveness. Resurrection is the means by which God bears witness to Jesus as the One whom God has sent. Beyond the narrative is the promise of a fulfillment when Jesus returns again. This is a complicated narrative, but it is narrative all the same.

What is strikingly missing from the long narrative sermons of Peter and Paul is the material we find in Luke 4 through Luke

21—the ministry of Jesus, his healing and his preaching. I think this is in part because in the narrative sections of Acts the apostles themselves prolong this part of the story. They do in Jesus' name what Jesus himself has done in the Gospel. That part of the story is recapitulated in the acts of the apostles more than in their sermons.

## The Good News of God's Deeds

I have suggested that in Luke–Acts we find the first clear sign that the term "gospel," *euaggelion,* may be identified explicitly with an extended narrative about Jesus, especially about his crucifixion and resurrection. And I have suggested that Luke gives us clues that narratives within the narratives (like the parables) also proclaim good news.

We close with one obvious addition to this: for Luke this narrative is not just a good story, it is good history. Whatever else the prologues of Luke and Acts may indicate, they also indicate that it is important for Luke not just to get his story right but to get history right. Luke's often remarked-upon attention to dates and rulers further suggests that for Luke the good news is in part good news about what God is doing in human history.

Much useful work has been done on the difference between writing ancient history and writing our own, and no one would argue that Luke sets out to be a historian according to modern canons of historicity. But there is also no evidence that Luke would be satisfied in claiming to have told an edifying story about an imaginary world. For him this is a story about the real God dealing with real history in the real world.

And while there has been much backing off from the enthusiasm of some years ago for Hans Conzelmann's certainty that Luke was worried about salvation history more than he was about eschatology or forensic justification, there is something to Conzelmann's claim.[9]

If Matthew becomes a model for the way in which Bonhoeffer understands good news, Luke seems to me a paradigm for the way H. Richard Niebuhr has understood history, seen through faith:

> In external history value means valency or strength. The objective historian must measure the importance of an event or factor by the effect it has on other events or factors in the series. . . . Not what is noblest in his sight but what is most effective needs to be treated most fully.
>
> In internal history, however, value means worth for selves; whatever cannot be so valued is unimportant and may be dropped from memory.
>
> As with value, so with time. In our internal history time has a different feel and quality from that of the external time with which we deal as exoteric historians. The latter time resembles that of physics. . . . In internal history, on the other hand, our time is our duration. What is past is not gone; it abides in us as our memory; what is future is not non-existent but present in us as our potentiality.
>
> . . . When the evangelists of the New Testament and their successors pointed to history as the starting point of their faith and of their understanding of the world it was internal history that they indicated. They did not speak of events, as impersonally apprehended, but rather of what had happened to them in their community. . . . They turned to a past which was not gone but which endured in them as their memory, making them what they were. So for the later church, history was always the story of "our fathers," of "our Lord," and of the actions of "our God."[10]

I think there is a danger, fueled both by historical disappointment and by one kind of dialectical theology, that we will no longer be willing to name God in the world or to point to God in history. We have painfully seen that we are not helped when people trying to name God in the world seem to misname God egregiously, or misread the world. Of course it is a risky claim that we can see gospel acted out in the lives of ordinary people, or more astonishingly in the fate of the principalities and powers. But it is at least equally risky to remove God from the earth God has created and to deny the sovereign Lord sovereignty over human history.

Luke's good news is good news about what God is up to in the real world and among real events. Our preaching needs to look at the real world and to claim real events as signs of God's good news.

## Good News for Hard Times

If we remember what everybody remembers about Luke, we are on our way.

We remember the nativity and God come close in human form, God's peace among those with whom God is well pleased. We remember that the gospel is always good news about this man.

We remember the good Samaritan and God active in human history, driving against all odds and sometimes against all appearances toward a reign where the world is turned upside down and the despised Samaritan is the model for the faithful servant.

We remember the prodigal son and God's forgiveness—for those who are far off and for those who are near; God's reconciling love bringing us to God's self and to one another.

There is one picture I will always carry from September 11. It is a story on the local news station, a young man from a town just down the road, home from the World Trade Center, where he worked. He is telling the horrible story of what he has seen in a town that used to be familiar but that turned in an instant into a far and terrifying country. His father, who came from home to meet him at the station, is hurrying along behind him, walking faster than a man my age ought to walk and breathing harder than he ought to breathe. And every twenty seconds or so the young man interrupts his awful dialogue and looks back and says: "Are you all right, Dad?"

And then again: "Are you all right, Dad?" And then to the reporters: "That's enough now; we just want to go home."

At the center of Jesus' famous parable the aging father comes running down the steps as fast as his legs will carry him and faster than his heart should bear, dashes down the road to welcome his son who he thought was lost in his own domestic tragedy; and if the son has any sense at all, when he is through giving his little repentance speech, he will say what he ought to say: "Are you all right, Dad?"

Even in Luke's parable the father is not really all right. He has had to give up a lot of wealth and pride to let his son go, and he gives up a lot of dignity and pride to welcome him home again.

And Paul knows what Luke may not quite get (you see, I can't let Paul go). Paul knows that in the larger story of which the prodigal is a part, in Jesus' own story, when the Father sends the Son into the far country to suffer unimaginable pain, in that story the Father never really is all right again. Never the same. Never unaffected.

Bearing the scar of his own loss through all eternity. Always sending the Son away for our sake; always running down the road to greet the Son, always running down the road to greet us who are Christ's adopted sisters and brothers.

There may be better news than that, but I have yet to hear it.

*Sermon*

# "Who Is This Fellow?"
# Friday Eucharist

## LUKE 15:1–10

### I.

Fridays in Marquand are hard on us Baptists. First of all, the Lord's Supper, which we know and love to celebrate—about once a month—gets dubbed "the Eucharist." Second, the trays with little cups full of Welch's grape juice that our Lord served to the disciples are replaced with chalices of wine. And, hardest of all for the preacher, the freedom of the Spirit gives way to the lectionary.

The truth is, I thought I'd lucked out this year, because I was told that the assigned Gospel reading for today was Luke 15. Terrific, I thought. I've got about twelve sermons on Luke 15, eight on the prodigal son and four on the older brother. I'd preached at least six of the prodigal son sermons before the chair of the trustees board stopped me after church. "I'm tired of hearing about that younger brother," he said. "I've tried to do what's right all my life. I identify much more with the older brother."

I soon discovered that about half the people in the congregation identify more with the older brother, so I added to my sermons a variety of homilies on the theme of staying at home and sometimes feeling aggrieved about not getting your due.

Identifying, of course, is the clue to the story of the prodigal son and/or the older brother. We love to hear the story and sermons on the story because we all identify with one sibling or the other—or both. And those of us who have learned to enjoy narrative preaching love to preach on the parable because it's the closest thing to a full-blown short story we've got in the New Testament, and because we get to ask

Preached at Marquand Chapel, Yale Divinity School, September 22, 1995.

ourselves the key question for any good narrative sermon: "With whom do we want the congregation to identify this week?"

## II.

But who can identify with the lost sheep or the missing coin? (The bad news, as you've just heard, is that this is what the lectionary assigns me, not the brothers with whom we can empathize so readily.) We haven't a clue to the internal life of a lamb or a drachma, either one. Does the sheep, having wandered far from the fold, come to itself and repent of its prodigality? Does the coin, in its isolated corner, notice that the other nine are having so much fun in the purse and regret its fake self-sufficiency? Of course not.

Our text this morning gives us no surrogate selves to help us with our issues of identity. We know nothing of the implicit or explicit faith of the sheep or of the penitence of the coin. They are not the subjects of the text nor the objects of our gaze. Luke in fact tells us what the issue is: "The Pharisees and the scribes were grumbling and saying, 'This fellow welcomes sinners and eats with them.'"

For now "this fellow" is the one we think about. The host at the table, not the guests. For now the issue is not sinners, sheep, or a coin—or us. For now the issue is: Who is this fellow? What does God do in him?

## III.

This fellow who eats with sinners is like a shepherd, leaving ninety and nine behind to seek out one. In the church of my childhood there hung a picture of the shepherd reaching out for the sheep. Somewhat hazy and haloed to be sure, a little romantic for my later taste, but what sticks in my mind is the fact that the shepherd was leaning precariously over the cliff to reach the sheep. As if, in seeking, the shepherd left not just the ninety-nine but his own safety behind—a quest almost foolhardy in its riskiness.

This fellow who eats with sinners is like a woman with ten silver coins, who loses one and turns the house upside down until she finds it. Maybe that's just prudence. If you've only got a dollar, every dime counts. But as you look at the story, what starts out looking frugal ends up looking nearly spendthrift. The woman lights every light. She sweeps and scrubs and scours and searches. All that oil burned, all that energy spent. A single-mind longing for the lost.

"Who is this fellow who eats with sinners?" our text asks. Not who are we, but who is he? Not what is it like to be a prodigal or an elder brother or a lost sheep or a missing coin, but who is the one who chases after sheep, crawls around looking for coins, heads out seeking daughters and sons?

## IV.

Beloved, this early in the semester and in our careers and in our lives, before we have had time to worry any more about our salvation or our vocation, and certainly before we begin worrying about our transcript, the gospel invites us to think on the one who saves us and the one who calls us. The gospel invites us to praise the one who alone in heaven or on earth deserves the highest honors God can give.

Even as we come to his Table, before we have much time for self-examination or self-doubt, we are invited to turn our gaze on Jesus, our host—in Eucharist, in thanksgiving.

For before you knew how to seek for anything, God in Christ was seeking you—like a foolhardy shepherd risking life and limb to reach a sheep, like a woman one coin short who diligently, passionately, won't give up until the lost is found.

Like an old father sitting on a porch who sees his child heading down the road, and not counting his dignity a thing to be hoarded, empties himself, hitches up his skirts or hitches up his trousers, scrambles down the steps and scurries down the road—to throw his arms around you, and to bring you home.

To Christ be thanks and praise.

## Chapter Five

# The Gospel of John

## The Gospel as Truth

Readers have always noticed that the Gospel of John represents a perspective unique among early Christian writings, and when we seek to discover John's understanding of what makes good news good, we find that uniqueness confirmed. The fourth Gospel simply does not use any of the terms that have been central to our discussions of Paul and the Synoptics—there is no use of the noun "gospel," no use of the verb "to preach the gospel" or "to evangelize," and no use even of the term "to preach" or "to declare."

Instead of "gospel" we find a pervasive emphasis on "truth," and instead of proclamation we find a pervasive emphasis on "witness." Running throughout the Gospel, binding concerns for truth to concerns for witness, is the stress on "belief."[1] Instead of the Synoptics' focus on the kingdom of God or Paul's focus on justification, adoption, and reconciliation, we find in John the central promise of eternal life.

Perhaps some of the uniqueness of the fourth Gospel can be found in the uniqueness of its social setting: a setting marked by its separateness both from the synagogue and from the larger church. I am persuaded by the work of J. Louis Martyn, Wayne Meeks, and Raymond Brown that a crucial context for the writing of the Gospel of John is a dispute between John's community and the larger community of the synagogue.[2] The story of the man born blind in John 9 becomes a kind of example story for Christian Jews on their way to becoming Jewish Christians. Like the man born blind, they are forced to choose between confessing Jesus and being cast out of the synagogue and denying Jesus in order to stay safe within the familiar, dominant community. It also seems clear, especially in the way that the fourth Gospel distinguishes its "beloved disciple" as source and authority from the less authoritative Peter, that the community of the fourth Gospel knows itself to be separate and distinct from the "mainline" church (I know the language is anachronistic) that looks to Peter—a church whose traces are perhaps most evident in the Gospel of Matthew.[3]

We have, therefore, in the fourth Gospel the testimony of a community that knows itself to be separate from a larger "world," or from two larger "worlds"—the world of the synagogue, out of which this community comes, and the world of the Petrine church, with which this community is in some competition.

The uniqueness of the Gospel's language is indicative of the uniqueness of the community's identity. The Gospel itself is written with terms and symbols that keep the Gospel self-referential, self-defining, puzzling to outsiders, revelatory to insiders.[4]

The literary strategy of the fourth Gospel works something like this: In chapters 2–11, in a series of dialogues, Jesus, who is the revealer of God and the representative of God's true community, provides, or seeks to provide, illumination to a group of characters who puzzle their way toward belief, or who fail to do so, or who puzzle their way in the general direction of belief—Nicodemus, the Samaritan woman, the man at the pool of Siloam, Mary and Martha. Interspersed with these educational dialogues are the disputes with those opponents who simply don't get it at all, sometimes called the Pharisees, sometimes called the leaders of the Jews, most often called just "the Jews."[5] Rudolf Bultmann says that the fourth Gospel relies on a "dualism of decision":[6] to choose for Jesus is to choose life; to choose against him, death. These dialogues and arguments distinguish between those who are moving toward choosing Jesus and those who have hardened their hearts to such a choice.

Chapters 14–17 consist primarily of a long monologue—in chap-

ter 17 a monologue turned prayer—in which Jesus seeks to explain
to those who have already become part of his community what such
membership entails. This last section of discourses is framed by the
action of Jesus' death and resurrection: supper in John 13, death in
John 18 and 19, resurrection in chapter 20. (Chapter 21 seems to be
a somewhat later addition to the original Gospel.)[7]

In each of these sections, in somewhat different ways, the
Gospel shows what it means to be part of this separated, unique
community. The first part of the book shows the meaning of faith;
the last discourses show the meaning of love in community; the
passion and resurrection narratives act out the meaning of loss
and life in ways that not only illumine Jesus' story but shape the
stories of those who believe in him.[8]

### Faith and Life: The Dialogues

In looking at good news in Matthew and Luke, I suggested that in
each case the last commission to the disciples provides a clue to
the good news the church is to proclaim (in Matthew, obedience
to God's righteousness; in Luke, forgiveness of sins). The end of
John's Gospel provides a clue, not so much to the mission of the
disciples, as to the mission of the book itself: "Now Jesus did many
other signs in the presence of his disciples, which are not written
in this book. But these are written so that you may come to believe
[in some authorities, "continue to believe"] that Jesus is the Messiah, the Son of God, and that through believing you may have life
in his name" (John 20:30–31).[9]

In a sense the book of John has become a sermon itself, its own
testimony to its own version of the truth. And these last verses
help us see three aspects of what John's truth might be: belief,
messiahship, and life.

### *Belief*

Two stories serve as examples of "coming to belief" in John's
Gospel.

The story of Nicodemus provides the most famous verse in all the New Testament, John 3:16: "For God so loved the world that he gave his only Son, so that everyone who believes in him may not perish but may have eternal life."

The story of Nicodemus's dialogue with Jesus is a story of what it might look like to come to belief (Nicodemus doesn't quite make it). Remember the social setting for this story. The Gospel is written to encourage Jews who are considering belief in Jesus to move toward full belief, even if it means separation from the world that has nurtured them, the world of the synagogue. Nicodemus represents not only the world of the synagogue, but its leadership. He comes to see Jesus by night. In the narrative world this reminds us that it is dangerous for a Jewish leader to show interest in this upstart, so he must not be seen visiting this teacher of Israel. In the symbolic world we remember the words in the prologue, John 1:5, a verse that can be read equally well in two ways: "The light shines in the darkness, and the darkness did not overcome it" and, "The light shines in the darkness, and the darkness did not comprehend it." It is clear enough in the Nicodemus story that Nicodemus does not overcome Jesus. Does he even begin to comprehend him?

The Nicodemus story itself, I think, depends on another pun, another double entendre. Jesus tells Nicodemus that in order to enter the kingdom of God, he must be born *anothen*. The Greek word can be translated two ways. Nicodemus must be born again; he must be born from above. From Jesus' explanation of his instruction, we know that the birth that awaits Nicodemus must be birth from above, given by the Spirit. "Do not be astonished that I said to you, 'You must be born from above.' The wind blows where it chooses, and you hear the sound of it, but you do not know where it comes from or where it goes. So it is with everyone who is born of the Spirit" (John 3:7–8). Jesus' explanation depends on another pun. The same Greek word can mean both spirit and wind, and I think Jesus' command to be born *anothen* depends on the pun, too. Nicodemus halfway gets the first half of the pun and misses the second half entirely.

Nicodemus halfway gets the first half of the pun because he knows that it looks like a ridiculous command— that he enter a second time into his mother's womb. But in the context of John's community, Nicodemus's coming to faith would be very much like being born again. The honors he had accumulated through his life would be worthless; his authority would be null and void; the synagogue, which was mother, father, sisters, and brothers to him, would not be his family any longer. In order to be born from above he would also need to be born again. Oddly, Christians today quoting the Nicodemus story most often quote the pun as "You must be born again," but interpret the pun as if it read only, "You must be born from on high," as if this were all a matter of spiritual experience, a quick visitation from heaven, Jesus in the heart and then on with life as usual. John's Gospel knows that birth from on high is a giving up as much as a taking on: the shaking of the foundations.[10] For John's community it was separation from the comfortable world of the synagogue that was demanded. In our time it may be the comfortable world of consumerism and acquisition that we are called to leave behind. (We return to John 3:16 when we talk about "life," and to puns at the end of the chapter.)

The story of the Samaritan woman in John 4 tells us something about Jesus' own journey before it tells us about the woman's journey toward faith. His willingness to ask a Samaritan woman for a drink shows what all the Gospels show from time to time, that his ministry is in part a matter of reaching out beyond the boundaries of tradition, gender, religion. Whether or not, as Raymond Brown suggests, the story reflects the ways in which the community behind the Gospel is learning to include Samaritans in its midst, it does show a sign of the way in which the ministry of Jesus is always seen as stretching the boundaries of God's community.[11]

Once again the movement toward faith depends on the right deciphering of a puzzle, hearing of a pun. Jesus promises to give the woman living water; she interprets this to mean running water or water from a spring, but he means water that gives life.

As the living water, as the spring of God's new life, Jesus nudges the woman toward faith. He performs a sign by revealing that he knows her marital status. John's term for miracles is "signs." The term reminds us that miracles always point beyond themselves. For John signs are a good start, but only a start toward faith. Then Jesus broadens the woman's vision of God, beyond the particularity of Samaritan or Judean worship to the worship of God in spirit and truth (spirit like the Spirit that could birth Nicodemus; truth to which the whole Gospel points in 20:31). Jesus broadens her eschatology to include not only the hour that is coming but the hour that now is.[12] She knows him as prophet; she suspects that he is Messiah. He leads her toward faith through dialogue: question, answer, misunderstanding, understanding. At the end of the dialogue the Samaritan woman leaves the water jar at the well, because she has received the water that lasts for eternity. She runs to tell others (in John the truest disciples bear witness). And the fullest faith comes from those whom she calls to come and see. They not only see, they hear. Not just on the basis of his signs but on the basis of his word they come to believe, and what they believe is not just that he is Israel's Messiah (the boundaries keep stretching), but that he is savior of the world.

"And many more believed because of his word. They said to the woman, 'It is no longer because of what you said that we believe, for we have heard for ourselves, and we know that this is truly the Savior of the world.'"[13]

## Jesus, Messiah, Son of God

As with the other Gospels, John's Gospel is greatly concerned to help us know who Jesus is. As Messiah he is the fulfillment of Israel's hope, though Israel may not know it. As Son of God he is the hope of the world, a remarkable claim for a sect largely ignored or rejected by the "world" it knew.[14] The Gospel claims this for him: He is the one who has come from the Father, and to the Father he will return.

The prologue to the Gospel presents in poetry some of the themes that will be explicated through narrative and discourse. Jesus' lineage is traced, not back to Abraham, as in Matthew's

Gospel, or back to Adam, as in Luke's Gospel, but to the very beginning of creation. The Word was present with the Father at the creation, and now the Word has been sent to dwell with the creation (John 1:14).

In one of his disputes with the Pharisees, Jesus makes clear his claim, at least to those wise hearers who understand his words:

> Even if I testify on my own behalf, my testimony is valid because I know where I have come from and where I am going, but you do not know where I come from or where I am going. You judge by human standards; I judge no one. Yet even if I do judge, my judgment is valid; for it is not I alone who judge, but I and the Father who sent me. (John 8:14–16)

He comes from the Father; he shall return to the Father. The story begins with the Word being sent to dwell among us. The story ends with his being lifted up on the cross, halfway toward home. For John theology is geography.

That Jesus is sent from beyond means that he transcends the world even while dwelling in the world. That Jesus is sent from the Father means that his words are not only his words but the Father's words, his authority is the authority of the one who delegated and sent him as an ambassador of life. That Jesus returns to the Father means that his mission is not validated by the acceptance or rejection of those who hear and meet him here, but by the welcome of the Father.

Implicit in all this is that those who read this Gospel and believe will know that this Jesus is not simply a man but the man from heaven and that his death is not defeat but return. Because they believe in him they will be in this world but not of this world. They receive their lives from him, and stake their lives on him precisely as the one who loves the world but comes from beyond and will return beyond, as well.

John's Gospel also claims this for Jesus. Jesus is the "I am" who reveals the fullness of the Father in the life of the community. Jesus' statements about himself often begin with the Greek phrase

*Egō eimi*, "I am." We might interpret this simply as a quirk of John's style until we note those places where the words obviously take on a richer connotation. In one case, Jesus is speaking to the Jews:

> "Your ancestor Abraham rejoiced that he would see my day; he saw it and was glad." Then the Jews said to him, "You are not yet fifty years old, and have you seen Abraham?" Jesus said to them: "Very truly, I tell you, before Abraham was, I am." So they picked up stones to throw at him, but Jesus hid himself and went out of the temple. (John 8:56–59)

The oddity of the use of the present tense "I am" and the reaction of Jesus' opponents suggest that what he says is not merely strange but blasphemous. The claim "I am" is more than a simple statement of identity.

Again toward the end of the story, when the soldiers and the police come to arrest Jesus he asks them:

> "Whom are you looking for?" They answered, "Jesus of Nazareth." . . . When Jesus said to them, "I am he *[Egō eimi]*," they stepped back and fell to the ground. (John 18:4–6)

Almost certainly the claim that angers some and fills others with awe is the claim that Jesus is identifying himself with the God who spoke to Moses from the burning bush: "But Moses said to God, 'If I come to the Israelites and say to them, "The God of your ancestors has sent me to you" and they ask me, "What is his name?" what shall I say to them?' God said to Moses, 'I AM WHO I AM *[Egō eimi ho ōn]*,'" (Exod. 3:13–14).[15]

As God revealed God's own self to Moses, so Jesus reveals God's own self in his words and in his deeds. And his words and deeds echo those of the Father from whom he comes. (In addition to the "I am" passages, see John 5:17.)

This helps us understand the power of those claims that permeate the Gospel: "I am the true vine." "I am the good shepherd." "I am the way, and the truth, and the life." The great discourse on the bread from heaven combines our two themes. Jesus is the one who is sent. Jesus is the revealer of God's own self. Here, as often, the revelation of who Jesus is follows after a sign pointing to that reality. The sign is the feeding of the five thousand. After some dispute about the meaning of this sign, Jesus compares himself to the manna that sustained Israel.

The crowd asks him, clearly missing the significance of the feeding:

> "'What sign are you going to give us then, so that we may see it and believe you? What work are you performing? Our ancestors ate the manna in the wilderness; as it is written, 'He gave them bread from heaven to eat.'" Then Jesus said to them, "Very truly, I tell you, it was not Moses who gave you the bread from heaven, but it is my Father who gives you the true bread from heaven. For the bread of God is that which comes down from heaven and gives life to the world." They said to him, "Sir, give us this bread always."
>
> Jesus said to them, "I am *[Egō eimi]* the bread of life. Whoever comes to me will never be hungry, and whoever believes in me will never be thirsty." (John 6:30–35)

In part in the speech that follows Jesus is trying to improve the crowd's exegesis. They read the story of the wilderness as if it were Moses who had given the people bread from heaven, but Jesus assures them that the "he" who gives bread is not Moses but the Father, God.[16] Nevertheless, the bread that God gave in the wilderness is only a foreshadowing of the true and greater bread that God sends in Jesus. The discourse now grows complicated, because the bread is associated primarily with Jesus' life-giving word, but secondarily with the bread of the Lord's Supper (see 6:56).[17] In either case (or in both cases) the Gospel makes this strong claim: the truest bread from God is not the manna but the bread that comes in Jesus Christ. Above all, through the word, but also through the sacraments, Jesus is the revealer of God's own self. He has the words that lead to life.

The invitation to life, of course, also presents the possibility of death. Rudolf Bultmann's dualism of decision shapes this story, too.[18] At the end of the discourse, "many of his disciples turned back and no longer went about with him. So Jesus asked the twelve, 'Do you also wish to go away?' Simon Peter answered him, 'Lord, to whom can we go? You have the words of eternal life'" (John 6:66–68).

### Life

I have suggested that "life" or "eternal life" functions in John's Gospel somewhat as "the kingdom" or "reign of God" functions for Matthew and Mark: life is the reality that Jesus reveals and to which he provides the way.

It is the story of Lazarus that makes most clear what "life" (and resurrection) signify in John's Gospel. It seems clear that John's Gospel shares the early Christian hope for life beyond the grave— whether in a final resurrection or an individual return to the Father we shall discuss below. However, it is also clear that Bultmann is right when he makes the case that John's Gospel also points to a kind of realized eschatology. Eternal life is not just life beyond this life but it is life in the present qualified by the light and mercy of the Eternal.[19]

In John 11 it is Martha who represents the traditional view of eternal life and Jesus who corrects her by providing a broader vision:

> Martha said to Jesus, "Lord, if you had been here, my brother would not have died. But even now I know that God will give you whatever you ask of him." Jesus said to her, "Your brother will rise again." Martha said to him, "I know that he will rise again in the resurrection on the last day." Jesus said to her, "I am *[Egō eimi]* the resurrection and the life. Those who believe in me, even though they die, will live, and everyone who lives and believes in me will never die." (John 11:21–26)

Here it is the present tense of the familiar phrase that carries particular weight. "I *am* the resurrection and the life." (Italics added.) Right here. Right now. The further expansion of that claim is a little confusing—can it really mean that believers never die? More likely, in typically Johannine puzzling language, Jesus insists that for the believer eternal life begins now and continues forever. The promise of eternity qualifies present life; the quality of life that begins now for believers continues beyond time.[20]

The NRSV, in its admirable attempt to be as inclusive as possible, uses plurals that make Jesus' assurance sound more communal than it is. More narrowly translated, 11:25–26 reads: "The one who believes in me and dies, shall live, and everyone who lives and believes in me will not die eternally." This last maintains the tension between present and future judgment and could be translated "will not enter into eternal death"—the terrible contrast to eternal life; death in the midst of life and nothingness beyond the grave. But the first part of the phrase is also significant: the one who dies shall live.

In Paul and in Matthew and Mark, the stress on the resurrection of believers is usually on the general resurrection; all the faithful will be brought to be with Jesus at the end of time. (The story of the thief on the cross in Luke sounds more like John's understanding of eternity. See Luke 23:43.) In John there is more the sense that at the time of his or her death the believer enters into that aspect of eternal life which continues beyond death.

> Do not let your hearts be troubled. Believe in God, believe also in me. In my Father's house there are many dwelling places. If it were not so, would I have told you that I go to prepare a place for you? And if I go and prepare a place for you, I will come again and take you to myself, so that where I am, there you may be also. (John 14:1–3)

The sense seems to be that on the death of the believer, Jesus will return and take her or him to the eternal abiding place with the Father. "Dwelling places" has the same root as the verb "abide," and John's Gospel is full of the promise of Jesus abiding with believers. Now the promise is reversed—believers will abide with him.[21]

In the light of John 11 and John 14, we can understand more fully the promise of John 3:16, which foreshadows almost exactly the themes of John 20:31:

"For God so loved the world that he gave his only Son, so that everyone who believes in him may not perish [that is, enter into that death which is forever] but may have eternal life," that is, life that bears the light of eternity now and that death cannot extinguish.

"These are written so that you may come to believe that Jesus is the Messiah, the Son of God, and that through believing you may have life in his name" (John 20:31).

I have testified that in my maturity Robert McAfee Brown helped persuade me to read the Bible with fresh eyes through his book *Unexpected News*.[22] In my youth he helped persuade me to read the Bible at all through his book for young people, *The Bible Speaks to You*. At the beginning of that book he tells the story of a navy chaplain, surely himself, who led a Bible study for his men on the eleventh chapter of John.

> When the discussion was over, a Marine corporal followed the chaplain back to his cabin. After a few false starts he got down to the point. "Chaplain," he said, "I felt as though everything we read this morning was pointed right at me. I've been living in hell for the last six months, and for the first time I feel as though I'd gotten free."
>
> As he talked, the story came out. He had just finished high school when he was called into the service. He had spent a long time in the occupation forces in Japan. He had gotten bored. Finally he had gone off one night with some friends and gotten into trouble. Serious trouble. . . . And he was sure God knew about it. He felt guilty, terribly guilty. . . .
>
> But somehow that wasn't the end after all. He kept repeating one idea over and over: "Up until today, Chaplain, I've

been a dead man. I have felt utterly condemned by myself . . . and by God. *I've been dead*, but now, after reading about Jesus and Lazarus, I know that I am alive again. The forgiveness of God can reach out even to me. The resurrection Jesus was talking about is a real thing, after all, right now."[23]

## Love and Community: The Discourses

It seems fair to say that the themes we've looked at—belief, messiahship, and life—dominate the first twelve chapters of John's Gospel. These are the themes that are illustrated and explored by the dialogues between Jesus and the woman at the well, Jesus and Nicodemus, and Jesus and Martha, and in the disputes of Jesus with his opponents, especially in John 6 and John 7. In John 14–17 the major rhetorical mode is not dialogue but monologue (in chapter 17 monologue as prayer), and the major theme is not so much coming to faith as life in community.

Harold Attridge has suggested that Bultmann's claim that in John's Gospel Jesus is the revealer, and that what Jesus reveals is precisely (and exclusively) *that* he is the revealer, is an oversimplification. The revelation does have further content. Jesus reveals the love of God through Jesus for the disciples, the community. And Jesus commands that the community show that love for one another.[24] We can see these themes developed in the final discourses.

### *Parables: The Love of God through Jesus*

John's Gospel does not work as the Synoptic Gospels do. Instead of good news we have truth, and instead of proclamation we have witness. Miracles become signs and they are the occasion for lengthy discourses rather than snappy pronouncements. In John as in the Synoptics there are parables, but the parables are full of detail, nuance, variation, complication, and perhaps even redundancy. Again one gets the sense of in-house language. It's not just that those who have ears can hear, it is that those who have learned the language may know how to interpret it.

Two parables show part of the content of Jesus' proclamation. Through Jesus, God brings the community into fellowship with God's self. The parable of the vine and the branches is part of the final discourses:

> I am the true vine, and my Father is the vinegrower. . . . You have already been cleansed by the word that I have spoken to you. Abide in me as I abide in you. Just as the branch cannot bear fruit by itself unless it abides in the vine, neither can you unless you abide in me. I am the vine, you are the branches. Those who abide in me and I in them bear much fruit, because apart from me you can do nothing. . . . As the Father has loved me, so have I loved you; abide in my love. If you keep my commandments, you will abide in my love, just as I have kept my Father's commandments and abide in his love. (John 15:1–10)

In discussing the nature of "eternal life," I have already suggested that the promise Jesus makes that in his father's house are many "abiding" places suggests that eternal life is life that abides in Jesus, both in this life and beyond death. In this parable Jesus makes clear that the love of God that abides in him is available to believers through him. The image of the vine is quite different from Paul's image of the church as the body of Christ in 1 Corinthians 12 and Romans 12. For Paul what makes church is in part the diversity and interdependence of the church members. For John what makes church is the dependence of each member (each branch) on Jesus (the vine). The unity of the church comes not so much from the interdependence of its members as from the fact that all share a dependence on Jesus. His love enables their love; indeed, their love is perhaps best understood as a manifestation of his.[25]

The other great parable occurs, not in the discourses, but toward the end of the more dialogical section of the Gospel (thus messing up my overly simple distinctions). This parable has some similarities to the shepherd parables of Luke 15:3–7 and Matthew 18:12–14. Here is a portion of the Johannine parable:

> I am the good shepherd. The good shepherd lays down his
> life for the sheep. . . . I know my own and my own know me,
> just as the Father knows me and I know the Father. And I lay
> down my life for the sheep. . . . For this reason the Father
> loves me, because I lay down my life in order to take it up
> again. (John 10:11–17)

Now it becomes clear, not just that community is constituted
by the love of the Father through the Son, but that community is
constituted by the Son's willingness to lay down his life for the
community's sake. The shepherd knows the sheep as the vine sus-
tains the branches, but more than that, the shepherd keeps the
sheep by his willingness to lay down his life for their sake.

### Commands: The Love of the Community

We can say that in John the "good news" so important to
Matthew, Mark, and Luke becomes "truth." I think we can also
say that the law, which is crucial to Matthew's understanding of
good news, in John becomes a single command, but for John as
for Matthew that command is also part of the "truth," part of the
good news, not alien to it.[26]

The first reference to a "command" in John's Gospel is reference to a command Jesus has received from the Father. It comes
at the end of the shepherd parable we have just heard: "No one
takes [my life] from me, but I lay it down of my own accord. I have
power to lay it down, and I have power to take it up again. I have
received this command from my Father" (John 10:18).

Just as the love of the Father for Jesus is transmitted and validated through Jesus' love for the community, so the Father's command to Jesus for sacrificial love is transmitted and validated
through Jesus' command to the community. This word comes at
the end of the other parable, the parable of the vine:

> This is my commandment, that you love one another as I
> have loved you. No one has greater love than this, to lay

down one's life for one's friends. You are my friends if you do
what I command you. . . . I am giving you these commands
so that you may love one another. (John 15:12–17)

If this is John's version of the Synoptic Great Commandment, it
is in some ways more narrow and in other ways more daring than
that more traditional word to love the neighbor as the self. It is
more narrow because it is quite clear here that the love demanded
of the believer is not the love of the neighbor in the larger world
but the love of the brother and sister in the communion of the
church. Our somewhat anachronistic language is that this is a
Gospel written for a sectarian community, and in that day as in
this one thing that makes sects sects (and that keeps sects strong)
is the central, almost exclusive attention to love within the community. The command is also more radical than the Synoptic
commandment, because it not only asks believers to love one
another as they love themselves; it asks them to love one another
as Jesus has loved them—even to the giving up of self for the
other's sake.

Perhaps that giving up of self will mean what it would mean for
Nicodemus: giving up the perquisites and privileges that validate
the self in its social context, for him the perks and privileges of
leadership in the synagogue. Perhaps that giving up of self will
mean what it means for Jesus, actually laying down one's life for
the sake of the community. We do not know what was in fact
demanded of believers in John's church; we do know that in John's
Gospel life comes through death, or through being born again. (I
return to this below.)

### Promise: The Paraclete as Guarantor of Community

In many and diverse ways the writers of the New Testament deal
with the fact that Jesus, who lived and taught and died and rose
again, is no longer physically present in the life of the community.
Matthew stresses the presence of Jesus in the life of the community, God with us. Paul stresses the way in which the church is the

body of the risen Lord. John brings comfort in his claim that in the absence of Jesus, God will send "another comforter." The Greek term is *paraclete*, and it can mean "comforter," or "instructor," or "advocate." Not surprisingly, in a Gospel where words often have multiple meanings, for John "paraclete" means all these things.

For John "paraclete" means all these things because the Paraclete becomes the prolongation of the presence of Jesus in the life of the community. Jesus himself is the first Paraclete and the Spirit the "other" paraclete—because Jesus has been comforter, instructor, and advocate, so will the Spirit be.

> If you love me, you will keep my commandments. And I will ask the Father, and he will give you another Paraclete, to be with you forever. This is the Spirit of truth, whom the world cannot receive, because it neither sees him nor knows him. You know him, because he abides with you, and he will be in you. (John 14:15–17)

Not only will the Paraclete prolong Jesus' mission; the Spirit will also replicate Jesus' relationship both to the world and to the community. The world will not receive the Paraclete; the community will abide with the Paraclete. The world has not received Jesus: "He came to his own creation, and his own people did not receive him" ( John 1:11, au. trans.). But he does abide with the community and the community with him, in the time of his ministry, beyond his ministry through the Spirit, beyond life in the heavenly abiding places:

> When the Advocate [Paraclete] comes, whom I will send to you from the Father, the Spirit of Truth who comes from the Father, he will testify on my behalf. You also are to testify because you have been with me from the beginning. (John 15:26–27)

Note the themes. The Paraclete is the Spirit. He will bring comfort by his presence, but the Paraclete will also bring truth, as Jesus has brought truth, the content of God's revelation to God's people. The Paraclete will testify as Jesus has testified and borne witness, and the Paraclete will inspire testimony in the believers. The believers have been with Jesus from the beginning, as Jesus, the Word, has been with God from the beginning. They too are sent, and he is present with them through the presence of the Comforter. The Father sends the Son who sends the disciples; but the disciples are not sent unaccompanied into the world. The Spirit is the gift of the Father and the Son for the upholding of the community.

Finally, the Gospel suggests that it is the Spirit that teaches the community, in continuity with the teaching of Jesus. It is not too much to see here the evangelist's claim that through the Spirit this Gospel itself is the continuation of Jesus' ministry: "I have said these things to you while I am still with you. But the Paraclete, the Holy Spirit, whom the Father will send in my name, will teach you everything, and remind you of all that I have said to you" (John 14:25–26).

In all these ways we can see that the parables and discourses serve to move the reader beyond the stress on individual faith in Jesus to the stress on life in community. Jesus' word not only inspires belief; it builds fellowship. Jesus dies not just for the sake of the world, but for the sake of the sheep. Jesus commands not just loyalty to himself, but loyalty to one another, loyalty even to death.

If our guess about the nature of the church that reads and hears John's Gospel is correct, then we can see again how essential this book is to undergirding and encouraging a community that is seeking to find its own identity over against the world of the synagogue and maybe over against the world of the "larger" church. The good news is that this struggling body of believers is Christ's true vine, Christ's own flock, called and permitted to imitate his love through their love for one another, strengthened by the Spirit, which has come to be their "other" comforter.

### *Witness: Testimony and Trial*

In discussing Luke and Acts, we saw Luke's strong emphasis on witness as "bearing witness." John places equal stress on the idea of witnessing, but here the emphasis is more on being a witness, as in a court of law.

"Now is the judgment of this world," says Jesus; "now the ruler of this world will be driven out. And I, when I am lifted up from the earth, will draw all people to myself" (John 12:31–32). In the case that Jesus brings against the ruler of this world, the case by which he seeks to draw all people to himself, he calls on a number of witnesses.

The first witness is John the Baptist. "John testified [witnessed] to him and cried out, 'This was he of whom I said, "He who comes after me ranks ahead of me because he was before me"'" (John 1:15). The significance of his testimony is made clear in what is surely the most straightforwardly negative confession in the New Testament: "[John] confessed and did not deny it, but confessed, 'I am not the Messiah'" (John 1:20). In the court scene the witness makes clear that he is not innocent, not the lamb who will take away the sins of the world.

God testifies in the great cosmic court scene: "And the Father who sent me has himself testified on my behalf" (John 5:37a). And Jesus himself joins in the Father's witness, so that, as in a good courtroom case, the Gospel can present the testimony of two witnesses: "Yet even if I do judge, my judgment is valid; for it is not I alone who judge, but I and the Father who sent me. In your law it is written that the testimony of two witnesses is valid. I testify on my own behalf, and the Father who sent me testifies on my behalf" (John 8:16–18). In the "worldly" court before Pilate, Jesus again testifies about the truth, and those who have been reading carefully know that he is himself the truth of which he speaks (John 18:37; 14:6).

Scripture bears witness: "You search the scriptures because you think that in them you have eternal life; and it is they that testify on my behalf" (John 5:39).

When Jesus finally departs to be with the Father, the Holy Spirit will come to bear testimony, and inspired by that Spirit the disciples, too, will speak the truth about Jesus: "When the Advocate [Paraclete] comes, whom I will send to you from the Father, the Spirit of truth who comes from the Father, he will testify on my behalf. You also are to testify because you have been with me from the beginning" (John 15:26–27).

Finally the book itself becomes a witness; we circle around to the end with which we began: "These are written so that you may come to believe that Jesus is the Messiah, the Son of God, and that through believing you may have life in his name" (John 20:31).

### The Passion Narrative: Life out of Death

These last discourses, John 14–17, are of course framed by the narratives of Jesus' activity during the last week of his earthly life—supper before, betrayal, trial, and crucifixion after, and then by the stories of the resurrection. In different ways the story of the meal and the story of the passion underline the meaning of the command to lay down one's life for the community, and the story of the resurrection underlines the promise of life in the Spirit and beyond death.

Chapter 13 acts out the theme of the final discourses: that the disciples are to live as Jesus lived, giving themselves for the sake of others, showing love for the sake of the community. After Jesus has washed the disciples' feet, he makes clear that this is a kind of living parable—their lives should show forth their understanding.[27]

> After he had washed their feet, had put on his robe, and had returned to the table, he said to them, "Do you know what I have done to you? You call me Teacher and Lord—and you are right, for that is what I am. So if I, your Lord and Teacher, have washed your feet, you also ought to wash one another's feet. For I have set you an example, that you also should do as I have done to you. (John 13:12–15)

Some churches take these words as every bit as much words of institution as the Synoptic (and Pauline) words about the bread and cup. Whether or not the command can cause us to rethink our liturgy, it is certainly written to help us rethink our lives. Washing one another's feet is a sign of bearing one another's burdens, loving one another as Christ has first loved us. Church becomes church, community becomes community, in mutual and loving service.

There are words in John 12 that provide a clue, not just to the larger meanings of John 13, but to the significance of the whole passion narrative in this Gospel:[28]

> Jesus answered them, "The hour has come for the Son of Man to be glorified. Very truly, I tell you, unless a grain of wheat falls into the earth and dies, it remains just a single grain; but if it dies, it bears much fruit. Those who love their life lose it, and those who hate their life in this world will keep it for eternal life. Whoever serves me must follow me, and where I am, there will my servant be also. Whoever serves me, the Father will honor." (John 12:23–26)

In Mark's Gospel Jesus dies in loneliness and abandonment; in Luke's Gospel he dies in trust. In John's Gospel he dies in triumph. We can put it mythologically: In John's Gospel Jesus comes from the Father and seeks to return to the Father. The crucifixion, which looks to the world like defeat, is really a lifting up, a raising toward heaven, glorification. We can put it theologically: In John's Gospel the only way to life leads straight through death. We can put it metaphorically: Unless a grain of wheat falls into the earth and dies, it remains a single grain; but if it dies, it bears much fruit.

The passion story in this Gospel is the triumphal story of Jesus' march through death toward life, of his choosing the death that is the condition of his glory.

Several details show the centrality of this claim for John's Gospel. Whether or not John knew any of the Synoptics, the details show his quite different understanding of the meaning of the cross.

When the Greeks come seeking Jesus and he proclaims the metaphor of the seed that needs to die to bear much fruit, he goes on to apply the image to his own passion in language that seems almost like a deliberate correction to the familiar story of Jesus' agony in Gethsemane. "Now my soul is troubled. And what should I say—'Father, save me from this hour'? No, it is for this reason that I have come to this hour. Father, glorify your name" (John 12:27–28). The troubled soul recalls the prayer in Gethsemane that the cup of suffering might pass from Jesus, but the call to glorify becomes a way of showing how Jesus accepts unhesitatingly the vocation of suffering that God has set for him.

Another detail in John's passion story suggests the centrality of Jesus' willful choice of crucifixion: "So they took Jesus; and carrying the cross by himself, he went out to what is called The Place of the Skull, which in Hebrew is called Golgotha" (John 19:16b–17). Whether or not the evangelist directly knows one of the Synoptic Gospels, he does know the tradition that another had carried Jesus' cross for him. He will have none of that: Jesus chose his fate and acted on it deliberately, proudly, carrying his own cross straight up that hill.

As the crucifixion draws to its close, "When Jesus had received the wine, he said, 'It is finished.' Then he bowed his head and gave up his spirit"(John 19:30). "It is finished" is another of those Johannine puns: it is over, but more than that, it is completed. My mission is complete. I have reached my goal. "He . . . gave up his spirit." This is not a passion narrative at all, but an action narrative. Jesus hands the Spirit to his Father.

Fred Craddock finds an image that captures this theme in John's Gospel beautifully. Perhaps coincidentally (though knowing Craddock, I doubt it), the image recalls Jesus' words to Nicodemus in John 3:14–15: "And just as Moses lifted up the serpent in the wilderness, so must the Son of Man be lifted up, that whoever believes in him may have eternal life."

> You don't just turn loose of life. Life is a very tenacious thing and will not give itself up easily. First time I ever realized that was while chopping cotton on a farm. I don't know if you know what chopping cotton is, but you're chopping every-

thing but the cotton. You're chopping the weeds and all. But there was a snake, which I killed, but then I had to keep chopping the snake, calling my father and saying, "I've killed the snake, but it won't quit wiggling."

He said, "Well, son, a snake won't die until sundown." I didn't know that. He said, "You hang it on a fence," so I picked it up with a hoe and put it over on a fence. Every once in a while I'd look over at the fence, and there was just the tail of the snake moving just like that, until sundown.

And Jesus said, "I'm going to turn it loose." But it was not a decision that was determined by his friends—they tried to oppose it—and it was not a decision determined by his enemies. He looked at them with a level gaze and said, "You're not taking my life; I'm giving my life." He was free.[29]

These stories are written that we might believe, and that believing we might have life in his name.

What we come to believe is that the way to life leads straight through death. What we come to believe is that it is only by giving up everything that we will gain everything. Jesus, in broad daylight, going to death, giving up his Spirit, stands in contrast to Nicodemus, who sneaks in by night and sneaks out again, giving up nothing and therefore, of course, losing everything. Jesus' loss is foreshadowed by the story of the man born blind who gives up the synagogue but gains his sight; it is foreshadowed by the story of Martha and Mary, who lose their brother only to have him restored as a sign of the power of Jesus, who is resurrection and life.

As resurrection and life he returns at the end of the story long enough to make clear that the cross is glory and that his brief return to the disciples is a way station on his eternal return to the Father. He returns long enough to breathe on them Spirit, which is the Paraclete, his ambassador as he has been ambassador for the Father. He returns long enough to show Thomas the wounds that are the sign of death and therefore the sign of life, and to elicit from Thomas the words that make him surrogate for the reader, the hearer: "My Lord and my God!" He returns long enough to restore Thomas and to pronounce the stronger blessing on those who will follow Thomas, generation after generation: "Jesus said to him, 'Have you believed because you have seen me? Blessed are those who have not seen and yet have come to believe'" (John 20:28–29).

## The Pun-filled Gospel

As Mark's Gospel depends on irony, John's Gospel depends on wordplay. Perhaps this is appropriate for a Gospel that begins with the Word become flesh and where faith so often comes through hearing. As Markus Barth observes:

> The homeliness of John's language does not exclude extensive play on the double-meaning of some words. Sleep may stand for death, blindness for stupid obduracy, seeing for knowing, anew for being from above, going up for readiness to be crucified. Misapprehensions are met by clarifications. A positive affirmation made in one line is often followed by a negation in the following parallel line. When two words such as water and spirit, believing and knowing, hearing and keeping are combined by the simple conjunction "and," they are used almost as synonyms; the second serves to explain the first unmistakably and does not add a totally new dimension or entirely different element.[30]

Perhaps the clearest parallel in more recent literature to what John did all those centuries ago is in the writings of John Donne, like the evangelist a preacher and a poet too, lover of words and of playing with them.

> I have a sin of fear, that when I've spun
> My last thread I shall perish on the shore;
> Swear by Thyself that at my death Thy Sun
> Shall shine as it shines now, and heretofore;

And having done that, Thou hast done,
    I have no more.[31]

    The power of the poem depends entirely on our ability to hear in two ways: "done" is also Donne, the poet's name. "Sun" is also Son, God's own Son, brightness begotten.

    In Mark, faith is partly a matter of seeing things two ways. In John, it is a matter of hearing both meanings of a word—sometimes to choose one meaning, sometimes to choose them both.

    "It is finished," Jesus cries from the cross.
    Maybe that means: "It's all over."
    Maybe it means: "It's complete."

    Jesus tells Nicodemus, "You must be born *anothen*."
    Maybe that means you have to start all over again.
    Maybe it means you have to rely on the Spirit.
    Maybe it means both.

    John's Gospel is always asking: "Do you get it?" If you do, and you believe it's true, you have eternal life.

    And though John never uses the phrase, we know that that is also good news.

*Sermon*

# Sermon for Good Friday

## JOHN 19

### I.

Notice that in John's Gospel, Good Friday is not a tragedy, it's a triumph. In Mark's and Matthew's Gospels Jesus cries the awful cry of abandonment: "My God, my God, why have you forsaken me?" In John's Gospel he cries the cry of victory: "It is finished," which means, "I did it."

Even the small details play the note of victory. In the other Gospels, the tired Jesus has Simon of Cyrene carry the cross up the hill. In John's Gospel the determined Jesus carries it all by himself. In going to Calvary he does what he wants to do, just when he intends to do it. "It is finished."

J. Louis Martyn, who lives just down the road, has written a good deal about John's Gospel and helps us understand why this journey from Bethany to the top of Calvary is presented without the slightest sign of Jesus' wavering or doubting. When John's Gospel was written, there was a struggle going on in the synagogues of John's community. For years Jews who believed that Jesus was God's Son and Jews who doubted it had worshiped side by side. They worshiped the same God, after all, and there were all those years of shared stories, and shared aunts and uncles. Then there was some kind of crisis, and the leaders of the synagogue decided that followers of Jesus were not good Jews after all, so they excommunicated Christians who were openly Christian, kicked them out of the synagogue.

This helps explain why some of the language about Jewish people in John's Gospel is so intemperate. It was a family feud between one group of Jews and another, and you know how it goes in family feuds. The rhetoric escalates, and charity goes by the board.

Preached at Battell Chapel, Yale University, April 10, 1998.

The synagogue crisis also helps explain why John tells the story of the crucifixion the way he does. Jesus is a sign of all the good that God promises to those who have the courage to confess Jesus and follow him. Jesus is also a sign of what courage looks like. You may have to give up everything you've cherished to be a Christian (just as Jesus has to lay down his very life). But the wonder is this: that when you are willing to give up everything you will also gain everything—purpose, hope, comfort, confidence—life that is really life.

Look at Jesus. He lost it all; he found it all. The cross, which looked like defeat, was really victory. "It is finished," he cries. "I won."

## II.

Losing everything in order to find everything; dying to your old life in order to find a new and better life. Jesus is the great example in John's Gospel, but when Jesus brings us to the foot of the cross, we recall other examples too.

There's Nicodemus. Nicodemus, a ruler of the synagogue. Top of the heap. King of the hill. CEO of the most important firm in town; or Sterling Professor of Judaica; or partner in the biggest firm. Pastor of Old First Church, Phi Beta Kappa, and president of Rotary, all rolled into one. Nicodemus, sneaking out to see Jesus at night because Jesus is the outsider, leader of the other party; sneaking out to see Jesus at night because there is some promise that Jesus offers, some prize that Nicodemus can hang up on his wall along with his diplomas and his honorary gavels and his picture with the governor.

"What little thing can I add to my life in order to be part of your kingdom?" he asks Jesus.

"You must be born again," Jesus says, which is just a polite way of saying, "You've got to die." Give up all the powers and perks and start all over again, psychologically naked as a newborn babe. You've got to die to it all. Pull out of the synagogue, which is your family and your power and your prestige and your self-esteem, and cast your lot with this dubious band of believers in this risky venture. Wander out of University Church to Zion Holiness Church, or out of Yale to some community college, or out of whatever makes you most comfortable to take that challenge that has absolutely nothing going for it—except the call of God.

Tell you the truth, we don't know if Nicodemus ever makes the hard choice. He pops up twice again in the story. Once he shows up in time to say some vaguely commendatory things about Jesus. This is a strategy that has the advantage of not actually forcing Nicodemus to *believe* in Jesus or to follow him. And at the end—just after the cry of triumph on the cross—Nicodemus comes forward with a hundred pounds of spices to embalm Jesus. He's come halfway out of the theological closet. The one who had come to Jesus by night now shows up in full daylight. But he still comes to embalm Jesus in the fear or hope that if Jesus stays dead, nothing more will be asked.

My God, Jesus had asked a lot of him. It is so hard. Dying in order to find life.

### III.

Losing everything in order to find everything. There is the Samaritan woman, too. If Nicodemus had to give up his distinction, she had to give up her distinctions. Jesus is walking through Samaria, foreign territory, enemy territory. A Samaritan woman comes to the well, and he asks her for a drink. She says the perfectly natural thing: "How is it that you, a Jewish man, ask for a drink from me, a Samaritan woman?" Perfectly natural to define ourselves against each other. Man versus woman; Samaritan versus Jew.

Perfectly natural to take pride in being the insider, Jew, male. But maybe equally natural to take pride in being the outsider. I know who I'm not. Not a male like you. Not a Jew like you. Not an oppressor like you.

Thank God we're not like the powerless, say the powerful—helpless and marginalized. Thank God we're not like the powerful, say the powerless—arrogant and bigoted. Some of us proud to be victors and some of us proud to be victims.

Jesus marches right past the distinctions. "Give me a drink from the well," he says, "and I'll give you a drink from God. Give me what I need, I'll give you what you need." He doesn't just cross the line between outsider and insider, he abolishes it.

The Samaritan woman doesn't give up yet. We love our distinctions because we have nurtured them so long. All right, skip gender, and skip race. I'll tell you what makes us different from one another. "We worship on the mountain. You worship in Jerusalem." The rock bottom, inescapable, inevitable distinctions of theology. One of us has got to be right, and one of us has got to be wrong. Proud of our orthodoxy or proud of our heterodoxy. Proud of our bishops or of our suspicion of bishops.

"Neither Jerusalem nor the mountain," says Jesus. Neither the creeds nor rugged individualism. Neither bishops nor just folk. "The hour is coming," he says, "when you will worship the Father in spirit and in truth." The spirit, which knows no distinctions, the truth that does not choose sides. "You've got to die to all those splendid categories," says this odd Jesus, "in order to find your life in God."

Soon after, the woman fades from sight. But before she goes, we see her hurrying among the Samaritans, urging them to come down and see this Jew. Forgetting her own distinctions and ignoring her own categories in order to introduce people to this amazing life.

In her own way, dying in order to give life.

## IV.

We don't know what had happened to the Samaritan woman by the time Jesus came to the cross. We do know what had happened to his mother and to the disciple called beloved. We do know what had happened to those two people who we may guess loved him most powerfully and mourned him most deeply. There they stood at the foot of the cross, as we are apt to stand in our grief and our love. Totally focused on the loss. Totally separate from one another.

"Is there any sorrow like unto my sorrow?" the mother asked herself, the disciple asked himself. Nurturing and cherishing what they had every right to nurture and cherish—their exclusive, overwhelming love for the one who was dying. Their absolute devotion to him.

And then he called them to die too. To die to their total attention to him and the singularity of their grief. "Woman," says Jesus; she looks up from her tears. He points to the disciple. "Here is your son." "Son," he says, and the disciple must look up too, "here is your mother."

Demanding the hardest death of all, the death of what we have every right to: Our individual devotion and our private griefs. The awful losses that no one can take away and that no one can understand. The relationship to a beloved companion or a beloved Savior that is ours and ours alone. Demanding that we die to that—not give it up, but transform it, transfigure it into love for the person who stands beside us. The one whose grief is not our grief but is grief just the same; the one who needs our love.

"If you really love me," says Jesus to his mother, "love him too."

"If you really love me," says Jesus to his friend, "love her too."

My God, Jesus asks so much of us. It is so hard, dying in order to find life.

## V.

"It is finished!" cries Jesus. A cry of absolute victory. All is lost; all is found.

"It is finished!" cries Jesus, and for him, for now, it is.

But not for them. Not for Nicodemus waffling or the Samaritan woman sharing the news, or for the mother and friend learning to make a life together.

"It is finished!" cries Jesus, and for him, for now, it is.

But not for us, either.

Trying to discover what pride and power we must give up if we are to be born again into a brand-new life. Trying to get beyond the little distinctions that give us our identity and our pride and our appalling divisions. Trying to get beyond the absolutely valid grief and loss that keep us to ourselves, keep us from noticing the other one who grieves beside us.

His arms outstretched in victory and loss embrace the world. Even when he's crucified, especially when he's crucified, he will not let us go.

My God, he asks so much of us.

My God, he gives so much to us.

Amen.

# Notes

## Introduction

1. Harry Baker Adams, *Preaching: The Burden and the Joy* (St. Louis: Chalice Press, 1996), 3.

## Chapter 1

1. Conversation with Adela Yarbro Collins; J. Louis Martyn, *Galatians: A New Translation with Introduction and Commentary*, Anchor Bible (New York: Doubleday, 1997), 128–32.
2. Brevard S. Childs, *Biblical Theology of the Old and New Testaments: Theological Reflection on the Christian Bible* (Philadelphia: Fortress Press, 1992), 235. In both Romans and the Septuagint the Greek verb is *euaggelizomai*. See also "gospel, Gospels" *HarperCollins Bible Dictionary*, ed. Paul J. Achtemeier (San Francisco: HarperSanFrancisco, 1996), 385–86.
3. Martin Luther, *Luther's Works*, vol. 54: *Table Talk* (Philadelphia: Fortress Press, 1967), 20, no. 146. "The Epistle to the Galatians is my dear epistle. I have put my confidence in it. It is my Katy von Bora."
4. Paul Schubert, *Form and Function of the Pauline Thanksgivings* (Berlin: Walter de Gruyter, 1939), 8.
5. Hans Dieter Betz, *Galatians: A Commentary on Paul's Letter to the Churches in Galatia*, Hermeneia (Philadelphia: Fortress Press, 1979), 25.
6. Martyn, *Galatians*, 125.
7. See Alan F. Segal, *Paul the Convert: The Apostolate and Apostasy of Saul the Pharisee* (New Haven and London: Yale University Press, 1990), 209.
8. I am grateful to Yon-Gyong Kwon, whose dissertation reminds us of this theme, though he argues strongly that the primary category for understanding the new relationship to Christ is that of being an heir, and that the notion of being adopted is secondary to that. "Eschatology in Galatians" (Ph.D. diss., King's College, the University of London, 2000).

129

9. Abraham J. Malherbe, *Paul and the Thessalonians* (Philadelphia: Fortress Press, 1987), 48–49.
10. Paul Tillich, "You Are Accepted," in *The Shaking of the Foundations* (New York: Charles Scribner's Sons, 1955), chap. 19.

**Chapter 2**

1. Adela Yarbro Collins suggests this possibility in her study of themes in Mark's Gospel, *The Beginning of the Gospel: Probings of Mark in Context* (Minneapolis: Fortress Press, 1992). She notes it explicitly on p. 18. Supporting the possibility also are Bas M. F. van Iersel, *Mark: A Reader-Response Commentary*, JSOT Supplement Series 164 (Sheffield: JSOT Press, 1998), 89–90; and M. Eugene Boring, "Mark 1:1–15 as the Beginning of the Gospel," *Semeia* 52 (1990): 47; the article is pp. 43–81.
2. Samuel Taylor Coleridge claimed that he was interrupted before he could finish writing "Kubla Khan" and could never find the right words to complete the poem. Critics have suspected that this was either a disingenuous explanation of a clever attempt to leave the poem open-ended or a frustrated rationalization for writer's block. See Robert F. Fleissner, *Sources, Meanings and Influences of Coleridge's Kubla Khan: Xanadu Re-Routed: A Study in the Ways of Romantic Variety*, Studies in British Literature, vol. 46 (Lewiston, N.Y.: Edwin Mellen, 2000), 8-9.
3. In his comments on an earlier draft of this chapter, Frederick Simmons persuasively suggested that Mark 1:1–16:8 may be the beginning of the gospel, that the vision of Mark 13 shows what the "end" of the gospel will be, and that the time of the reader is the time of proclamation, between the beginning and the end.
4. Robert Fowler's use of reader response criticism in *Let the Reader Understand* (Minneapolis: Fortress Press, 1992), helps pave the way for this kind of reading. Van Iersel has a very similar reading of the relationship of the title of the Gospel to its ending in *Mark*, 507–8.
5. Some of the earliest manuscripts do not include "Son of God" as part of this opening verse.
6. Paul Tillich, *Systematic Theology* (Chicago: University of Chicago Press, 1951–1963), 3:103. The larger discussion is pp. 102–6.
7. James E. Dittes, *The Church in the Way*, 164. The chapter is an elaboration on this theme.
8. Paul Tillich, "Heal the Sick; Cast Out Demons," in *The Eternal Now* (New York: Charles Scribner's Sons, 1963). Available online at http://www.religion-online.org. The sermon was originally addressed to graduating students at Union Theological Seminary, New York, in 1955.
9. Ched Myers, in *Binding the Strong Man* (Maryknoll: Orbis, 1988), is one of the most powerful interpreters of Mark as a kind of political theology. On this passage see especially pp. 190–94. I am sometimes amused that

interpreters who are so sure that contemporary politics can't possibly be what Mark had in mind when he told this story are made less uncomfortable by the fact that, say, the Presbyterian Church is almost certainly not what Mark had in mind, either. Which doesn't mean there isn't something here both for the oppressed and for Presbyterians, and for oppressed Presbyterians.

10. William Wrede, *The Messianic Secret*, trans. J. C. G. Greig (Altrincham, England: St. Ann's Press, 1971). Originally published as *Das Messiasgeheimnis in den Evangelien*, 1901. Unlike many later interpreters, Wrede does not attribute this device to Mark, but to the pre-Markan tradition.

11. T. A. Burkill, *Mysterious Revelation* (Ithaca, N.Y.: Cornell University Press, 1963).

12. In fact in her fascinating book *Sowing the Gospel* (Minneapolis: Fortress Press, 1989), Mary Ann Tolbert suggests the ways in which this parable provides the clue to the puzzle of Mark's entire Gospel.

13. Martin Kähler, *The So-Called Historical Jesus and the Historic Biblical Christ*, trans. Carl E. Braaten (orig., 1896; Philadelphia: Fortress Press, 1964), 80, n.11.

14. Susan R. Garrett, *The Temptations of Jesus in Mark's Gospel* (Grand Rapids: Wm. B. Eerdmans Publishing Co., 1998), 132.

15. I'm grateful to Frederick Simmons for this formulation. Garrett notes something of this theme in Mark, ibid., 132.

16. In Philip P. Hallie, *Lest Innocent Blood Be Shed: The Story of the Village of Le Chambon and How Goodness Happened There* (New York and London: Harper & Row, 1979), 257–58.

17. But see the oddly contrasting Mark 10:28–30.

18. Frederick Buechner, *Godric* (New York: Atheneum Publishers, 1980), 171.

19. Rudolf Bultmann, *History and Eschatology* (Edinburgh: University Press, 1957), 151–52.

20. The attempt to interpret this as a prediction of the transfiguration, which follows immediately, seems to me unconvincing.

21. E. L. Doctorow, *City of God* (New York: Plume/Penguin, 2001), 252–53.

22. Leander Keck points out that this verse may reflect the reticence in Jesus' own teaching: "Jesus did, however, expect God to act soon, though he was even more silent about the 'when' than about the 'what'; the saying about his not knowing the day or hour (Mk. 13:32) simply draws an appropriate conclusion from the fact that the tradition contained nothing about the time of God's expected action or about the length of the time span between Jesus' activity and God's decisive act—probably reflecting the memory that Jesus had said nothing about it" (*Who Is Jesus? History in Perfect Tense* [Columbia: University of South Carolina Press, 2000], 109).

23. Myers, *Binding the Strong Man*, 101. In order to keep its apocalyptic promise, the hope for the oppressed cannot finally be hope for this world only, either. The kingdom is and is yet to come. For helpful reflections on preaching apocalyptic, see Thomas G. Long, "The Preacher and the Beast: From Apocalyptic Text to Sermon," in *Intersections: Post-Critical Studies in Preaching*, ed. Richard L. Eslinger (Grand Rapids: Wm. B. Eerdmans Publishing Co., 1994), 1–22.

24. Wayne C. Booth, *A Rhetoric of Irony* (Chicago: University of Chicago Press, 1974), 30.

25. See Booth, *A Rhetoric of Irony*, 17; Robert M. Fowler, *Loaves and Fishes*, SBL Dissertation Series 54 (Chico, Calif.: Scholars Press, 1981), 93–99.

26. See Robert Fowler, *Let the Reader Understand*, 61 and passim. This term also originates with Wayne Booth, as noted in Fowler's citations.

27. C. Clifton Black, "Christ Crucified in Paul and in Mark: Reflections on an Intercanonical Conversation," in *Theology and Ethics in Paul and His Interpreters*, ed. Eugene H. Lovering Jr. and Jerry L. Sumney (Nashville: Abingdon Press, 1996), 184–206.

28. Patrick Henry, *The Ironic Christian's Companion: Finding the Marks of God's Grace in the World* (New York: Riverhead, 1999), 1–2.

29. Graham Greene, *The End of the Affair* (New York: The Viking Press, 1961), 116–17.

## Chapter 3

1. Ulrich Luz, *Matthew 1–7*, trans. Wilhelm C. Linss (Minneapolis: 1989), 197–98.

2. John Calvin, *New Testament Commentaries*, trans. A. W. Morrison, vol. 1 (Grand Rapids: Wm. B. Eerdmans Publishing Co., 1972), 169.

3. William Muehl, *Why Preach? Why Listen?* (Philadelphia: Fortress Press, 1987), 71.

4. In reading this over, Frederick Simmons reminded me that the "Decalogue" is ten "words," not ten "commandments"—and I would add that Torah is instruction as much as law.

5. See, for instance, W. D. Davies, *The Setting of the Sermon on the Mount* (Cambridge: Cambridge University Press, 1964), 309; Eduard Schweizer, *The Good News according to Matthew*, trans. David E. Green (Atlanta: John Knox Press, 1975), 16; Günther Bornkamm, "End Expectation and Church in Matthew," in *Tradition and Interpretation in Matthew*, ed. G. Bornkamm, Gerhard Barth, and Joachim Heinz Held, trans. Percy Scott (Philadelphia: Westminster Press, 1963), 20.

6. See Benjamin W. Bacon, *Studies in St. Matthew* (New York: Henry Holt, 1930), 80–90.

7. See Stanley Hauerwas and William Willimon, *Resident Aliens: Life in the Christian Colony* (Nashville: Abingdon Press, 1989), 24–29.

8. Paul S. Minear, *The Good News according to Matthew: A Training Manual for Prophets* (St. Louis: Chalice Press, 2000), 162.

9. Martin Luther, *Works*, vol. 21, *The Sermon on the Mount (Sermons) and The Magnificat*, ed. Jaroslav Pelikan (St. Louis: Concordia Publishing House, 1956), 10.

10. Luz, *Matthew 1–7*, 211–13.

11. Frederick Buechner, *Telling Secrets* (San Francisco: HarperSanFrancisco, 1991), 49–50.

12. See C. H. Dodd, *The Apostolic Preaching and Its Developments* (reprint, Grand Rapids: Baker Book House, 1980), 7.

13. Dietrich Bonhoeffer, *The Cost of Discipleship*, rev. ed., trans. R.H. Fuller (New York: Macmillan Company, 1949; 2d ed., 1959), 47.

14. Nicholas Wolterstorff, *Lament for a Son* (Grand Rapids: Wm. B. Eerdmans Publishing Co., 1987), 84–86.

15. In Günther Bornkamm, "The Stilling of the Storm in Matthew," in *Tradition and Interpretation in Matthew*, 55.

## Chapter 4

1. Rudolf Bultmann, *Theology of the New Testament*, trans. Kendrick Grobel (New York: Charles Scribner's Sons, 1951–55), 1:33.

2. Is Luke following Mark's outline here? If so, the synagogue sermon takes the place of the brief summary in Mark 1:15.

3. Robert McAfee Brown, *Unexpected News: Reading the Bible with Third World Eyes* (Philadelphia: Westminster Press, 1984).

4. In *The New Interpreter's Bible*, vol. 9 (Nashville: Abingdon Press, 1995), 229.

5. Frederick Buechner, *The Final Beast* (New York: Seabury Press, 1967), 114–15.

6. Gene E. Bartlett, *The Audacity of Preaching* (New York: Harper & Row, 1962), 86–87.

7. Sharon H. Ringe, *Luke*, The Westminster Bible Companion (Louisville, Ky.: Westminster John Knox Press, 1995), 289.

8. Thomas G. Long, *The Witness of Preaching* (Louisville, Ky.: Westminster/ John Knox Press, 1989), 44.

9. Hans Conzelmann, *The Theology of Luke*, trans. Geoffrey Buswell (New York: Harper & Row, 1961), 146–49, 161.

10. H. Richard Niebuhr, *The Meaning of Revelation* (New York: Macmillan Co., 1967), 67–72.

## Chapter 5

1. Brevard Childs, citing Rudolf Schnackenburg, points out that the fourth Gospel uses the verb "to believe" *(pisteuein)* 98 times compared with 11 for Matthew, 14 for Mark, and 9 for Luke. See Brevard S. Childs,

*Biblical Theology of the Old and New Testaments: Theological Reflection on the Christian Bible* (Minneapolis: Fortress Press, 1992), 608.

2. See J. Louis Martyn, *History and Theology in the Fourth Gospel*, 2d ed. (Nashville: Abingdon Press, 1968, 1979), 38–39; Wayne A. Meeks, *The Prophet-King* (Leiden: E.J. Brill, 1967); Wayne A. Meeks, "The Man from Heaven in Johannine Sectarianism," in *In Search of the Early Christians*, ed. A. Hilton and G. Snyder (New Haven, Conn.: Yale University Press, 2002), 55–90; and "Equal to God," ibid., 91–105; Raymond A. Brown, *The Community of the Beloved Disciple* (New York: Paulist Press, 1979), 40–43.

3. See Brown, *Community*, 81–88.

4. On this see Meeks, "The Man from Heaven," 59, 77, and note 16 on p. 82.

5. Some have argued that the term ought to be translated "Judeans," and is a geographical more than a religious designation. See Bruce J. Malina and Richard L. Rohrbaugh, *Social-Science Commentary on the Gospel of John* (Minneapolis: Fortress Press, 1998), 44–46; Malcolm Lowe, "Who Were the *Ioudaioi?*" *Novum Testamentum* 18 (1976): 101–30. Whatever the case about that, the text as it is read and heard in churches today remains an all too easy source of misunderstanding about Judaism, and at its worst of chronic anti-Semitism. Preaching on John (as on Matthew) needs from time to time to address this problem head on.

6. Rudolf Bultmann, *Theology of the New Testament*, trans. Kendrick Grobel (New York: Charles Scribner's Sons, 1951–55), 2:21, 76.

7. See, for instance, Francis J. Moloney, S.D.B., *The Gospel of John*, Sacra Pagina (Collegeville, Minn.: Liturgical Press, 1998), 545–47.

8. I'm inclined to agree with Brown and Meeks that the Gospel was written for those already "inside," but the early dialogues find ways of expressing the shape of coming to belief that got them "inside" in the first place. George Parsenios in a recent dissertation points out that thematically the first section of the Gospel deals with the descent of the Son and the second section with his ascent to the Father ("Departure and Consolation: The Polyphony of Genres in John 13–17" [Ph.D. diss., Yale University, 2002], 82–84).

9. I agree with many students of this Gospel that chapter 21 is an appendix added sometime after the writing of the first twenty chapters. While that chapter provides its own insights into the community that produced and used this book, the end of chapter 20 is a better clue to what goes on in the chapters that precede it.

10. David Rensberger sees that this birth requires a social relocation. *Johannine Faith and Liberating Community* (Philadelphia: Westminster Press, 1988), 54–57.

11. Brown, *The Community of the Beloved Disciple*, 35–40.

12. See Moloney, *Gospel of John*, 133.

13. In John 4:50 note how the official believes the word before he sees the sign. See Moloney, *Gospel of John*, 154.
14. I am almost persuaded by D. A. Carson that the clause should be read: "that you may believe the Messiah, the Son of God, is Jesus." "If this conclusion is sound, it means that the writer conceives of his purpose . . . less as the answer to the question 'Who is Jesus?' than as the answer to the question 'Who is the Messiah? Who is the Son of God?'" "The Purpose of the Fourth Gospel," *Journal of Biblical Literature*, 106/4 (1987): 643–44. The article is pp. 639–51. It fits well with such passages as John 7:27, 40–44.
15. For a somewhat different explanation of the *ego eimi*, see Moloney, *Gospel of John*, 273.
16. See Peder Borgen, *Bread from Heaven* (Leiden: E. J. Brill, 1965), 61–69, 172.
17. Rudolf Bultmann has persuaded many that this is a sign of redaction of the text: the earlier form of the Gospel stressed the life-giving word; a later, more sacramental, editor added the material about bread and wine. See Bultmann, *The Gospel of John*, trans. G. R. Beasley-Murray, R. W. N. Hoare, and J. K. Riches (Philadelphia: Westminster Press, 1971; orig., 1964), 219.
18. See note 6, above.
19. "For if God is the sole reality, then *life* is simply openness to God and to him who makes God manifest . . . 'eternal life' is equivalent to 'life'; the terms are used interchangeably by John." Bultmann, *Theology*, 2:19. For similar theme see also p. 34 and idem, *Gospel of John*, 258, 435, 494–95.
20. For a discussion of this dual aspect of "eternal life" in the fourth Gospel, see C. H. Dodd, *The Interpretation of the Fourth Gospel* (Cambridge: Cambridge University Press, 1953), 144–50. Dodd may see more of Plato in the background to the concept than I think likely, but presents well the balance between present and future life.
21. See Moloney, *Gospel of John*, 394.
22. See page 133, note 3.
23. Robert McAfee Brown, *The Bible Speaks to You* (Philadelphia: Westminster Press, 1955 reprint, 1984), 12.
24. Harold Attridge, in conversation. The Bultmann claim is in *Theology*, 2:66.
25. Ernst Käsemann understands Johannine ecclesiology in much this way in *The Testament of Jesus: A Study of the Gospel of John in the Light of Chapter 17*, trans. Gerhard Krodel (Philadelphia: Fortress Press, 1968; orig. 1966), 30–31.
26. I am not claiming here that John deliberately revises Matthew, though there are points, especially in the passion narrative, where I do think John deliberately revises some version of the Synoptic story. As with Matthew,

John wants to see in Jesus both continuity and discontinuity with the Old Testament, and especially with Moses.

27. When we read John with the Synoptics in mind, it remains odd that at the Last Supper there are no words of institution. Perhaps he deliberately uses the discourse about the bread of life and the true vine to lift up word and community over sacrament as the meaning of life together. Or maybe he is not deliberately dropping anything—simply telling a different kind of story.

28. Paul Minear sees that the footwashing in 13 and the reference to the dying seed in 12 together help interpret the story of the passion and its significance for believers, in "The Promise of Life in the Gospel of John," *Theology Today* 49 (October 1992), 491. The article is pp. 485–98.

29. Fred B. Craddock, *Craddock Stories*, ed. Mike Graves and Richard F. Ward (St. Louis: Chalice, 2001), 46.

30. Markus Barth, "Ultimate Reality and Meaning in the Light of John's Gospel," in *Ultimate Reality and Meaning* 12 (1989): 85. The article is pp. 84–103.

31. John Donne, "A Hymn to God the Father" (ll. 13–18), in *John Donne's Poetry*, ed. A. L. Clements (New York: W. W. Norton & Co., 1966), 94–95.